Desert Dreams
by
Emma Lilico Kinnear

www.emmalilicoart.com
Instagram @emmalilico
@eliliauk

ISBN-13: 978-1977734556

ISBN-10: 1977734553

For my Mum and my Granny, who are the most amazing, supportive, inspirational and powerful women in my life.

Dear Reader,

Following the positive responses and enjoyment people found within my first colouring book, I was asked to complete a second book. Having done plenty of research into Africa for my first book, African Savannah, it became apparent to me that there are lots of weird and wonderful creatures specifically local to Egypt. Not only does Egypt house some really amazing aniamls, but it also has a really rich history of architecture, language, and religion. These different aspects of Egypt have been incorporated in my designs, giving you both a connection to nature and a connection to rich culture as you colour.

My first book was inspired by my Grandpa, as he had always been a keen wildlife photographer. Two years ago he was diagnosed with Stage Four Lung cancer, which took a huge toll on myself and my family. He was well loved, and will be well missed. During the time that he was unwell, I was his full-time carer and the drawings from African Savannah gave me an escape from the sad reality. Since his death, my Granny has shown such strength and bravery, and immense support in absolutely everything I have done. It is because of her that I have motivation to keep creating, inspiring me and helping me to believe in myself.

ELILIA (www.emmalilicoart.com) is a business I have set up featuring my designs on tshrits and other merchandise. My aim is to raise as much as possible, to save the animals I draw from harm. My focus is anti-poaching, which unfortunately still happens all over Africa, and is incredibly under-funded. Many of the animals in this book are resourceful and resiliant and beautiful. Such rarity should be celebrated and cherished, not poached for commercial gain. Therefore, 10% of profits from this book and all over websites from ELILIA (www.emmalilicoart.com) are donated to organisations to assist in the protection of our wonderful animals from poaching.

Thank you so much for purchasing this book, and I hope you find as much pleasure and connection with Egypt as I did in creating it. Thank you for also supporting anti-poaching through your purchase.

Acknowledgements

Jane Muir
Dr. Susan Kinnear
Andrew Kinnear
Tom Chatterton
Owain Hughes
Katharine Preston
Hannah Baird

Thank you so much for your support and assistance

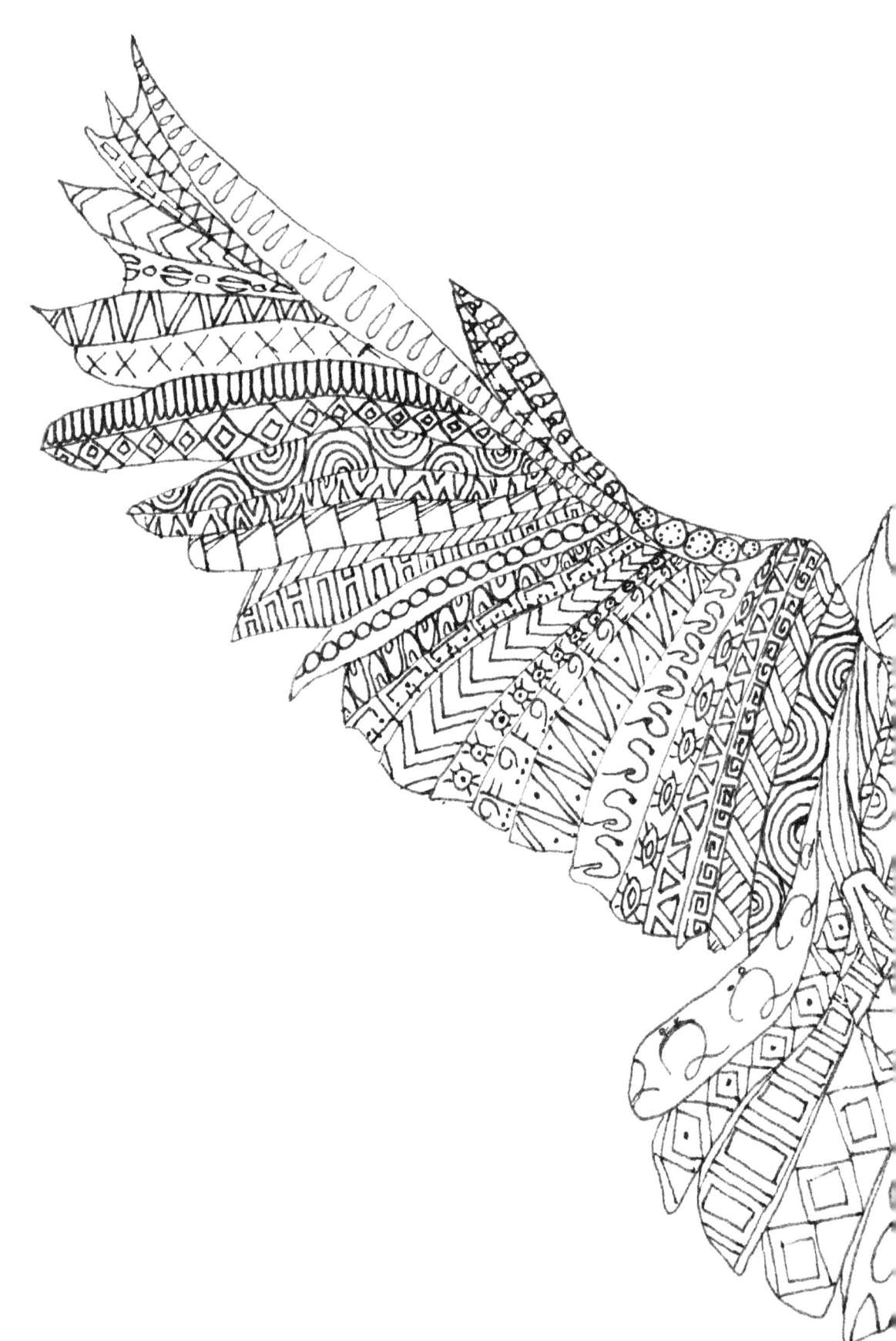

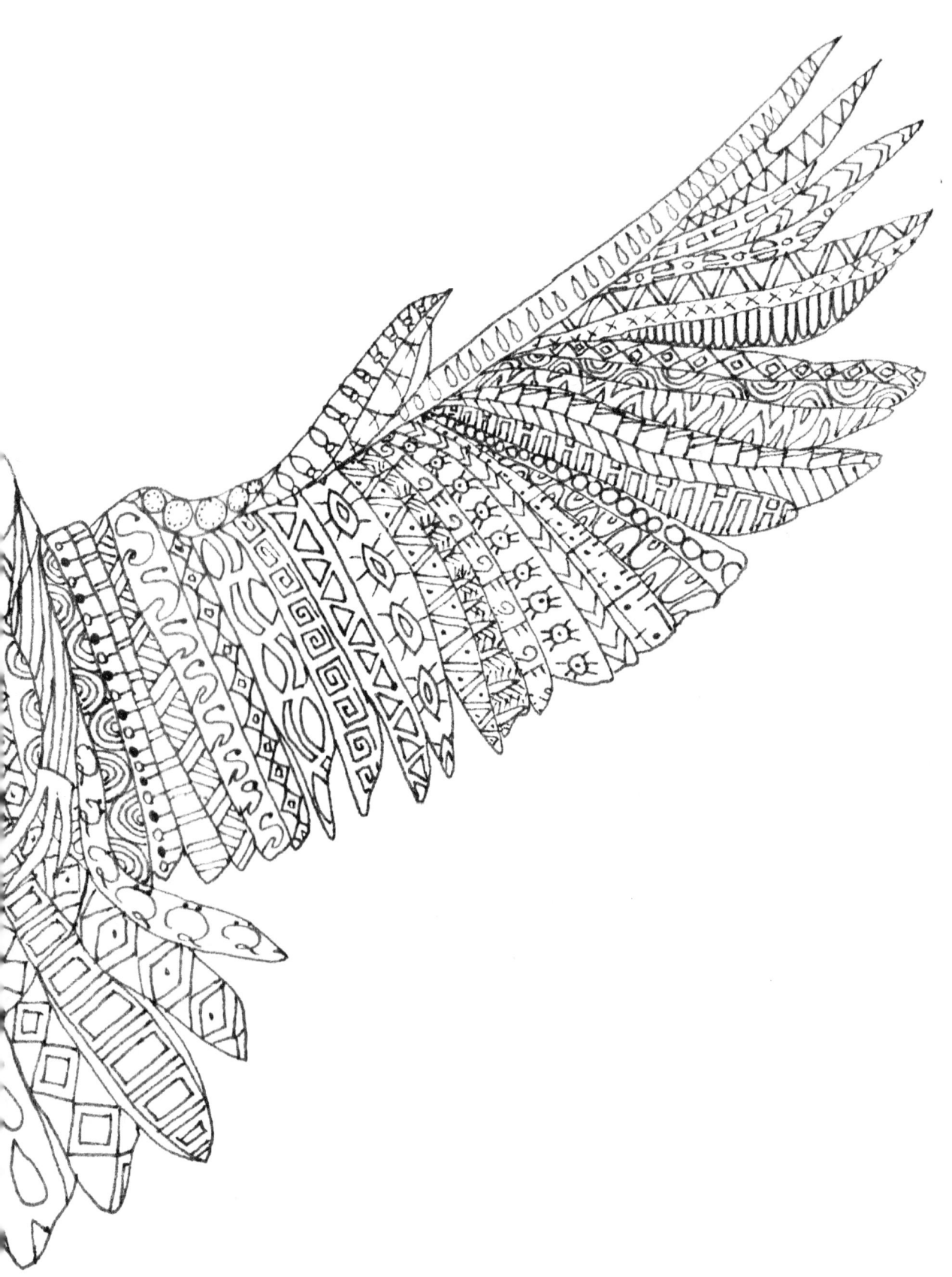

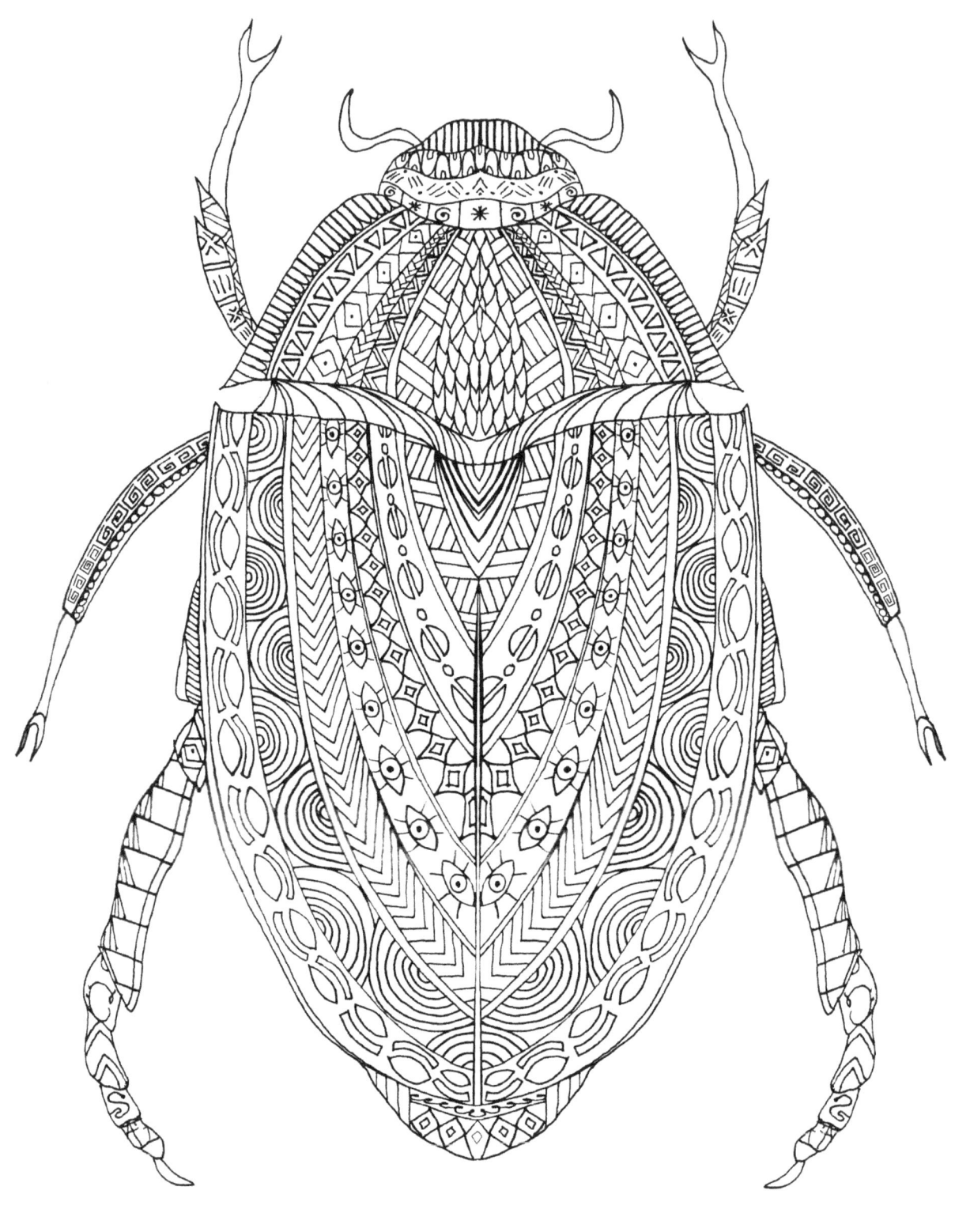

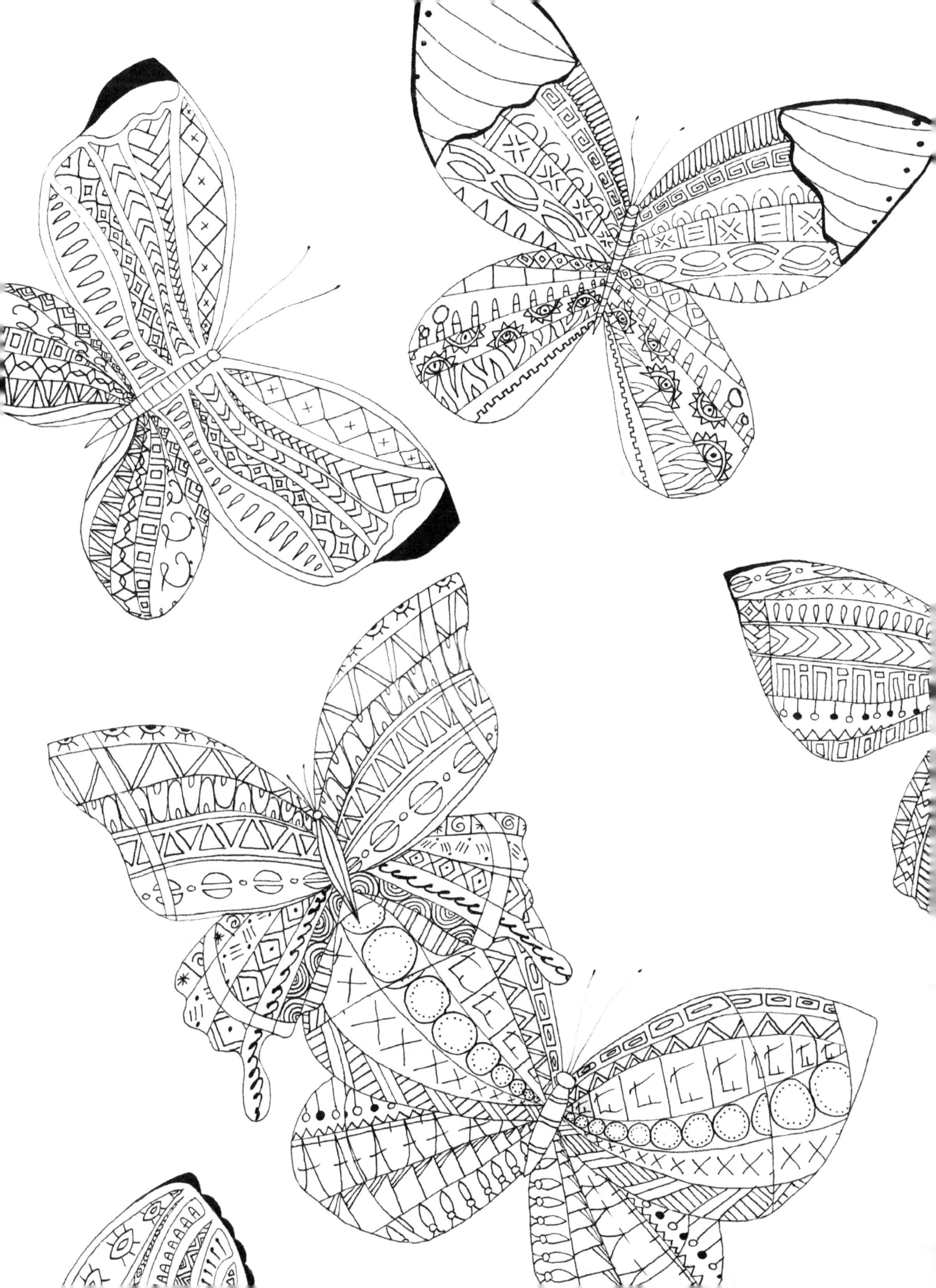

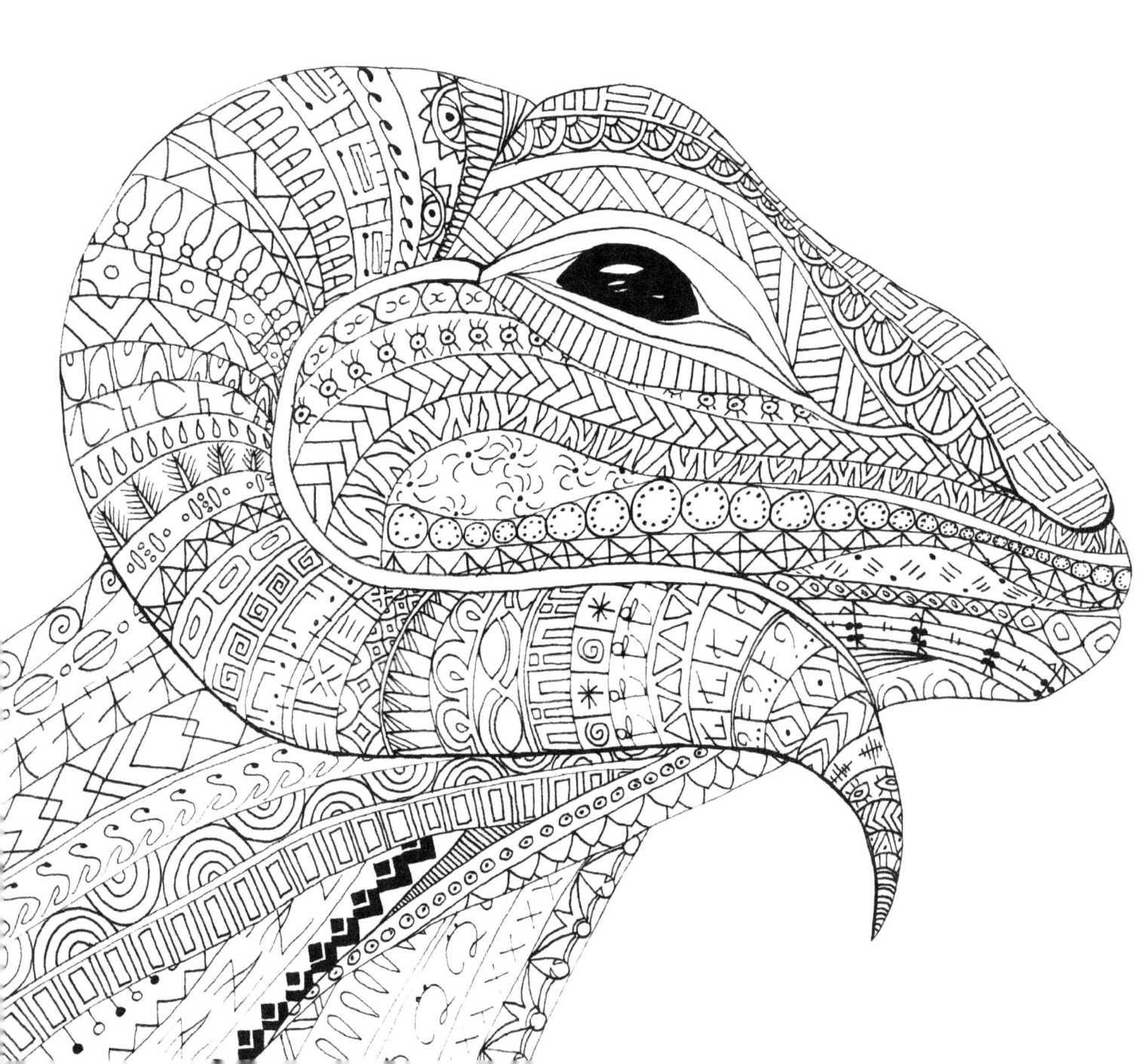

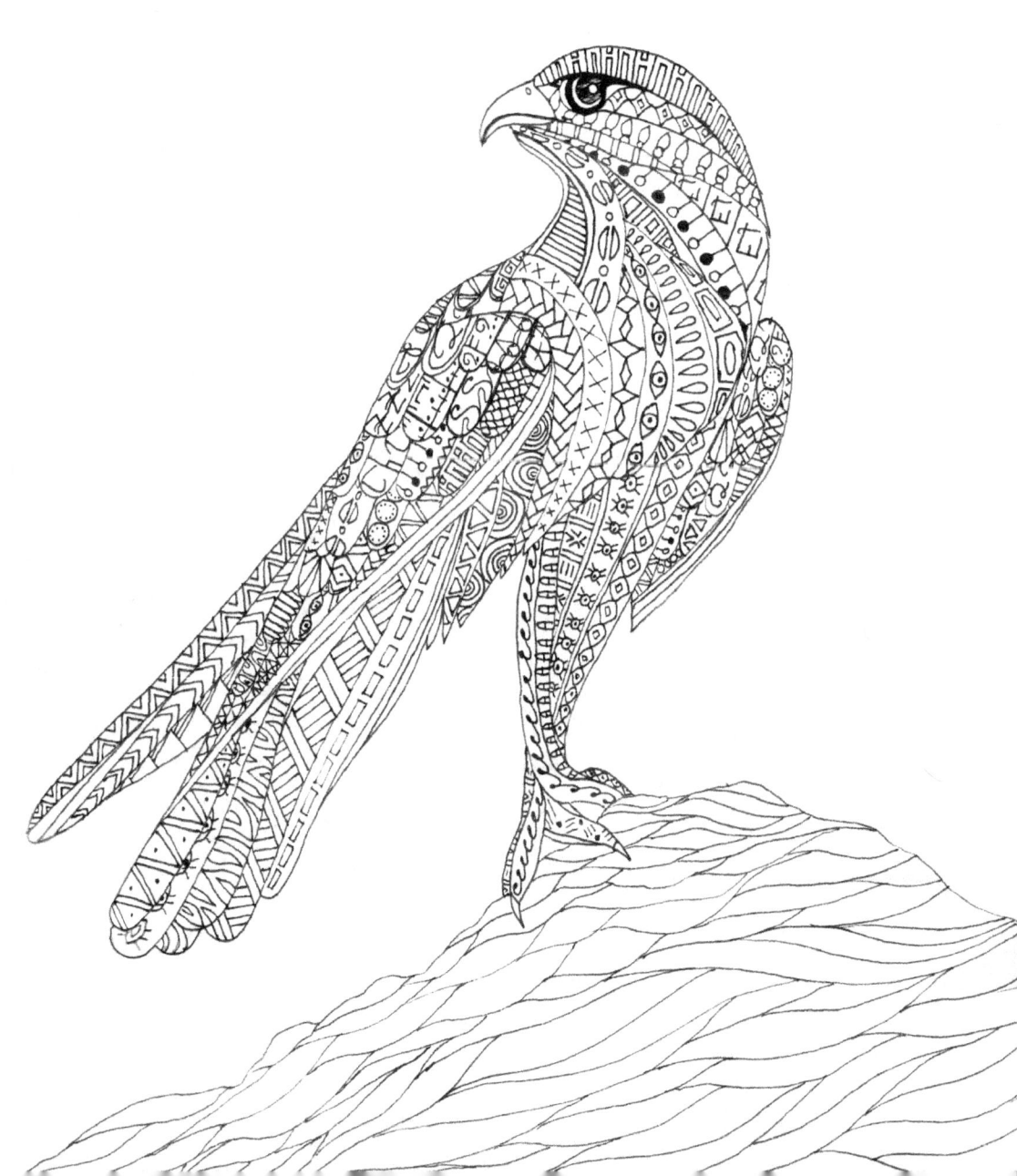

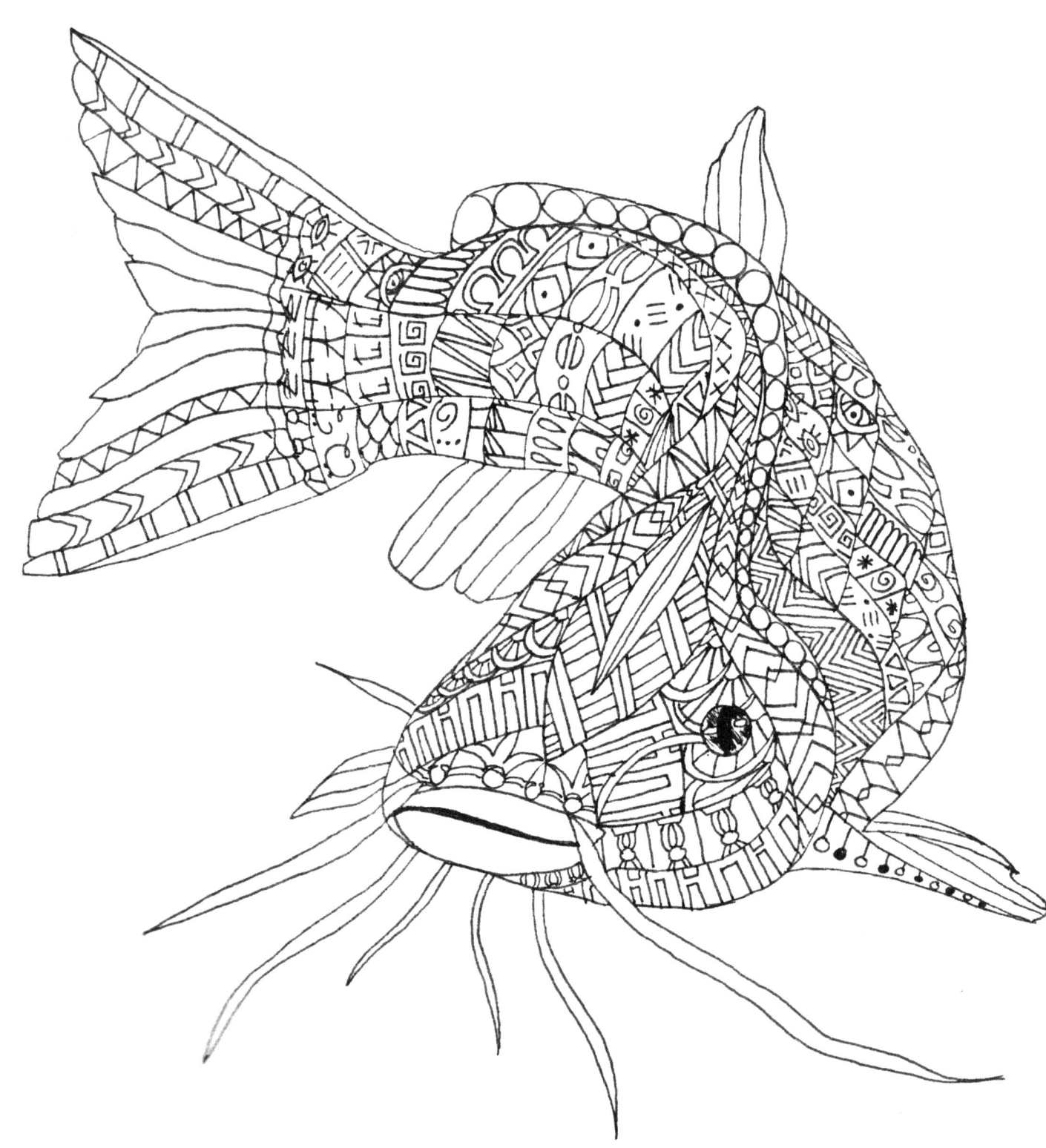

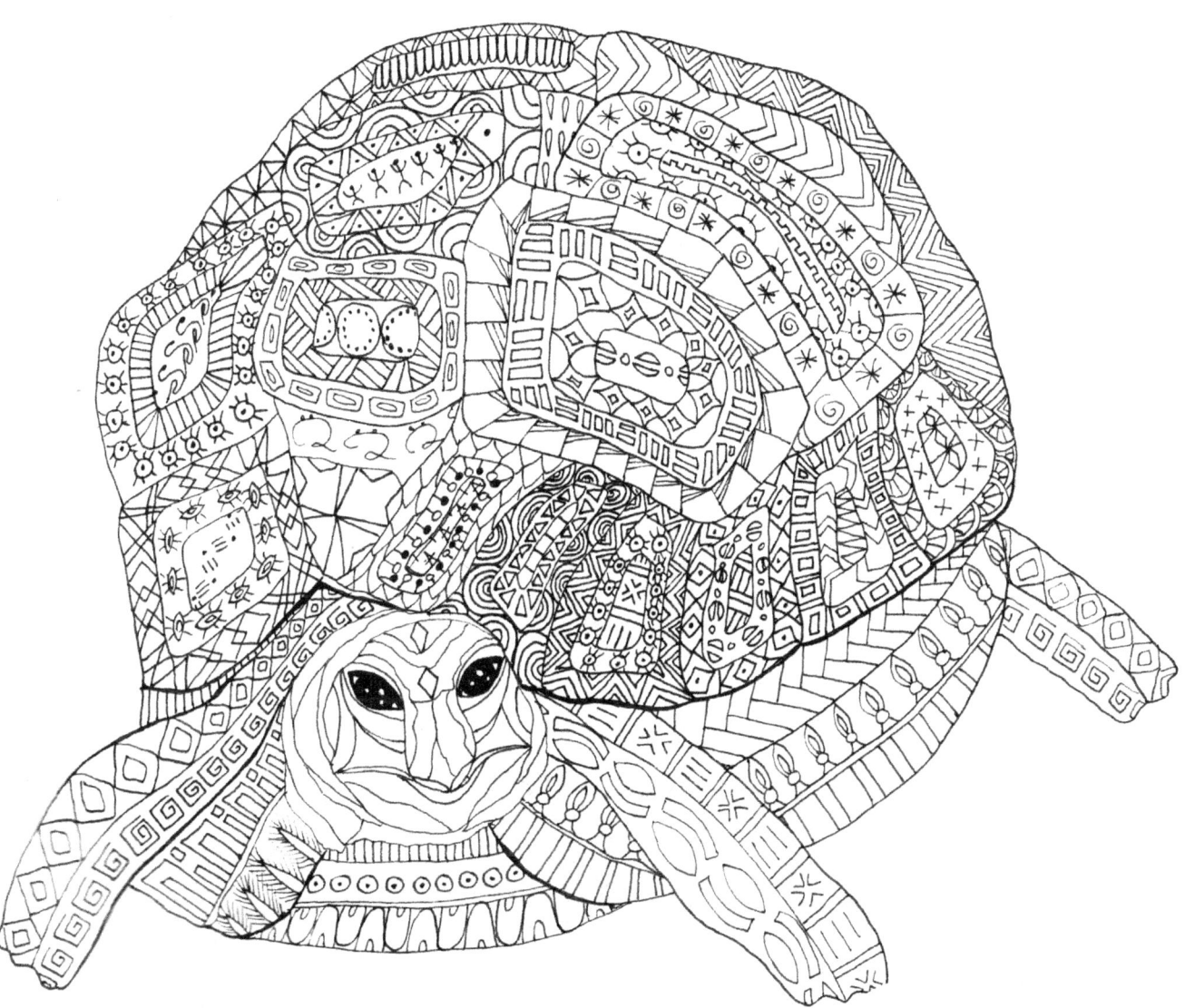

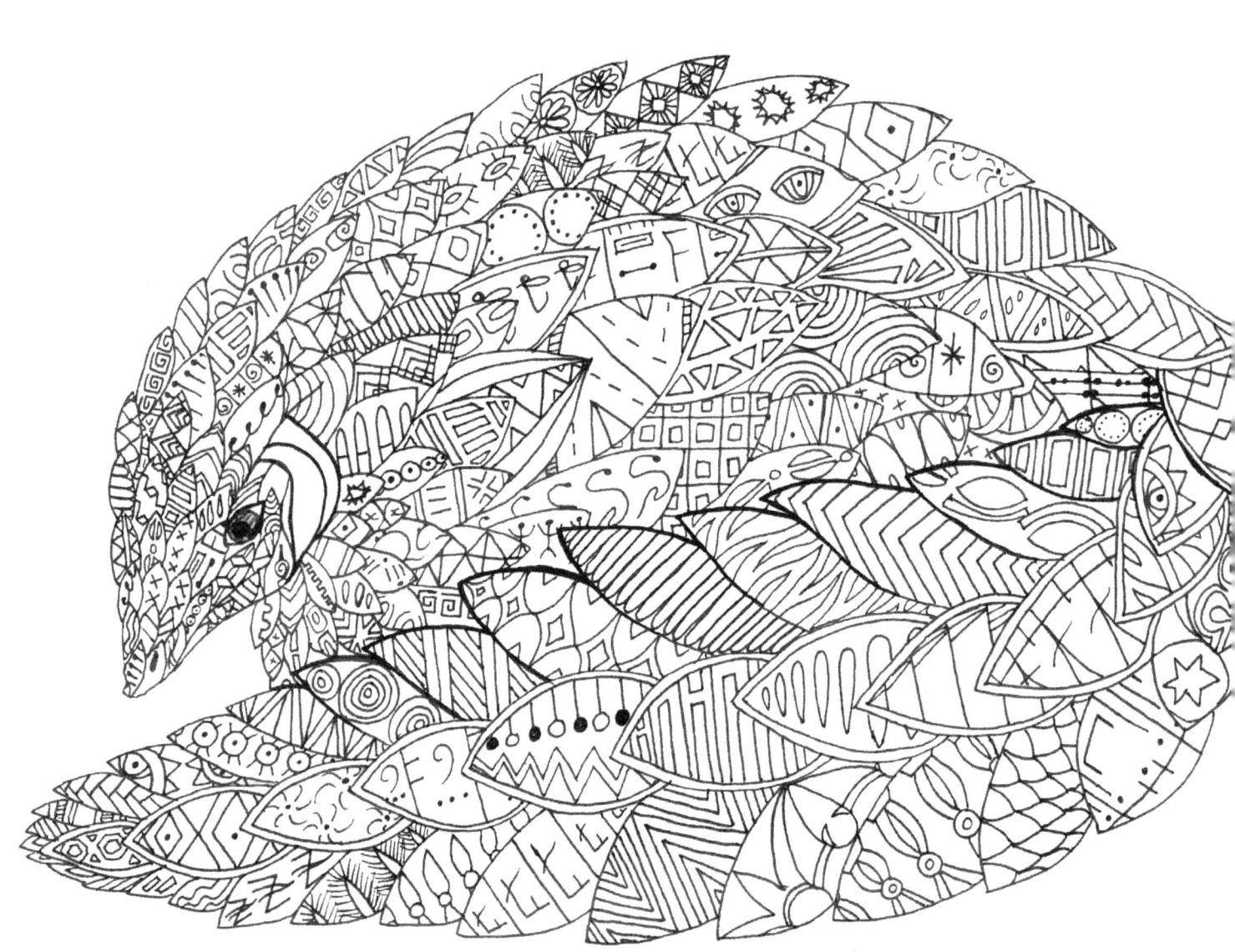

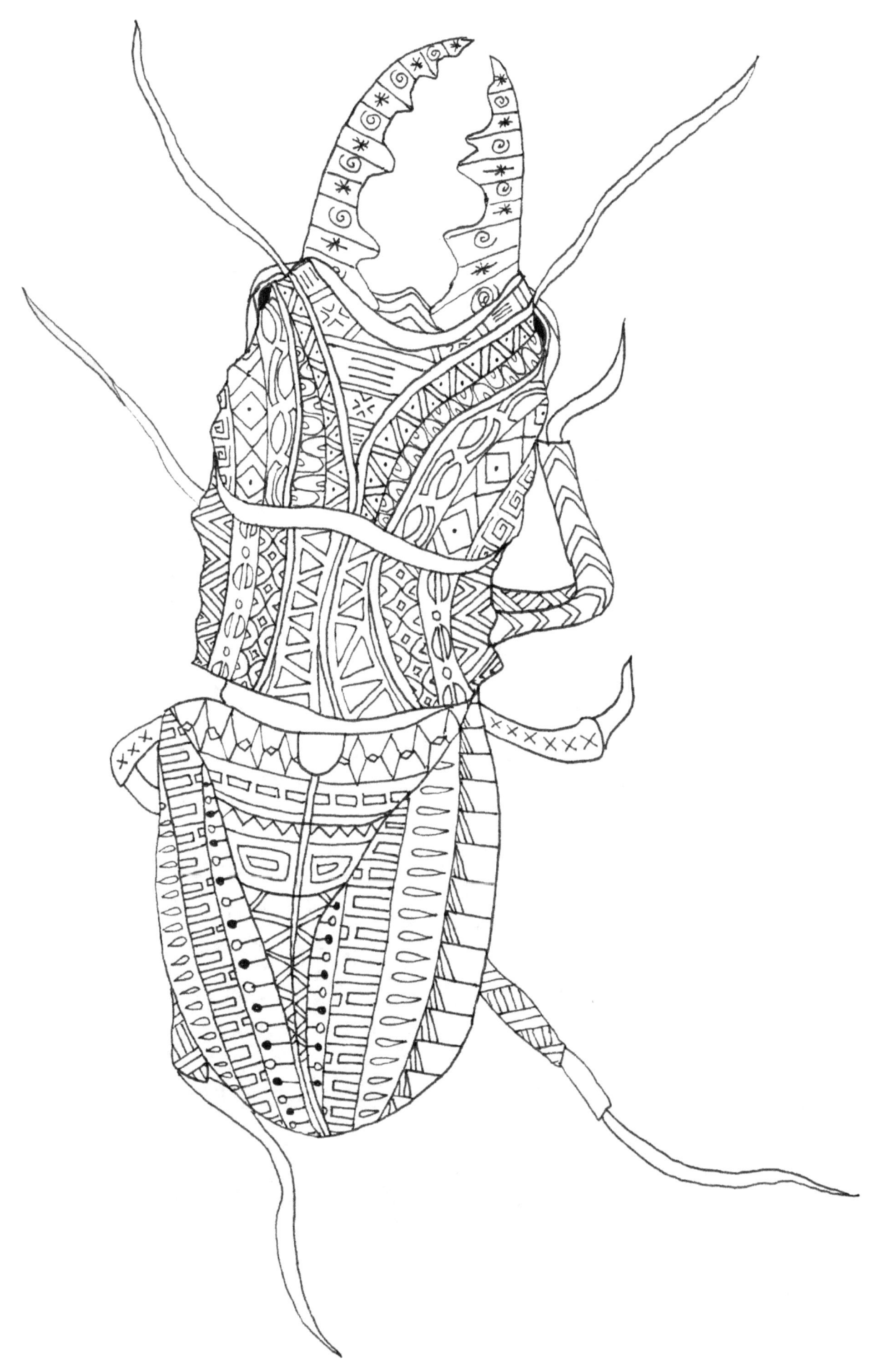

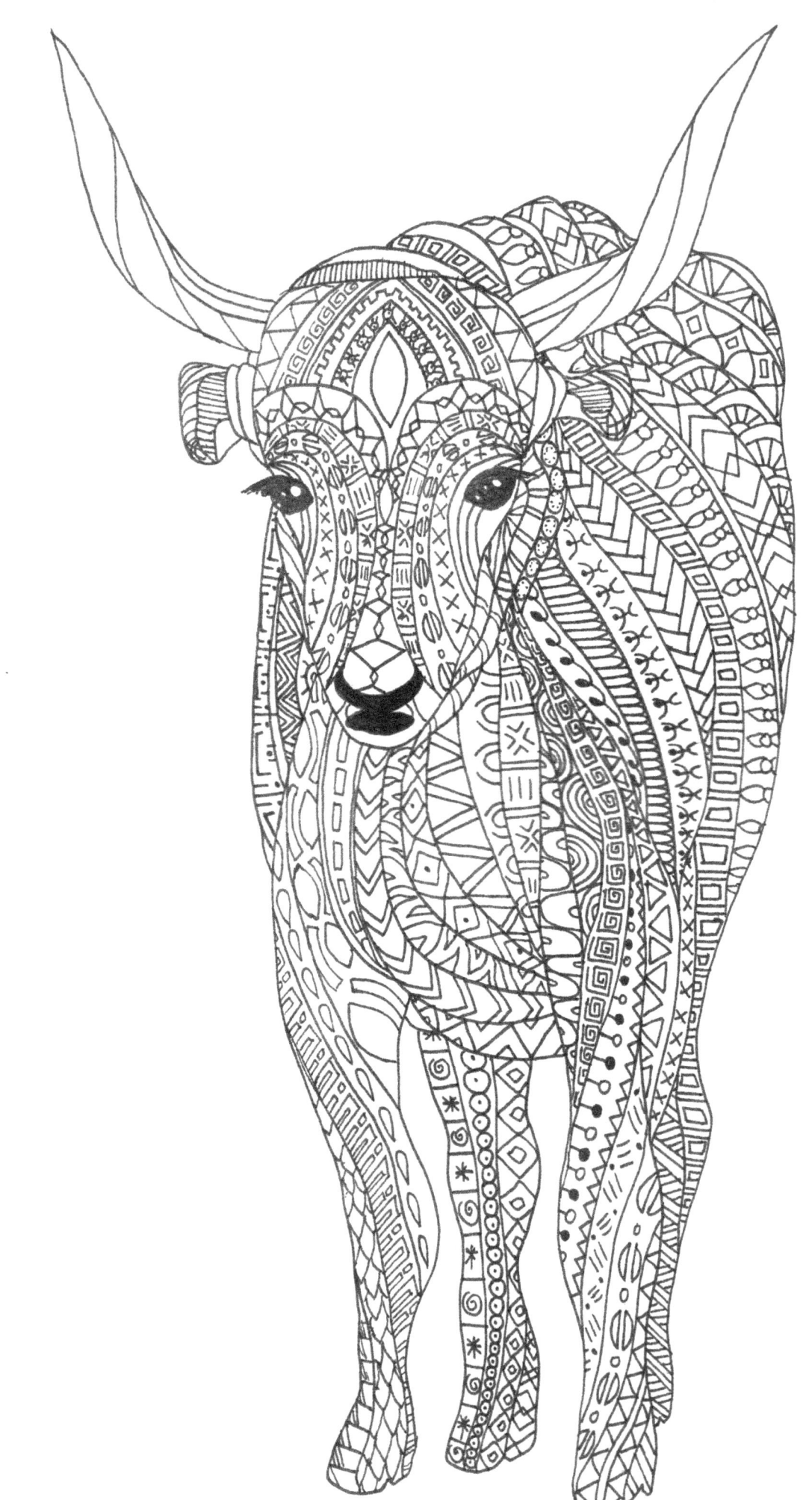

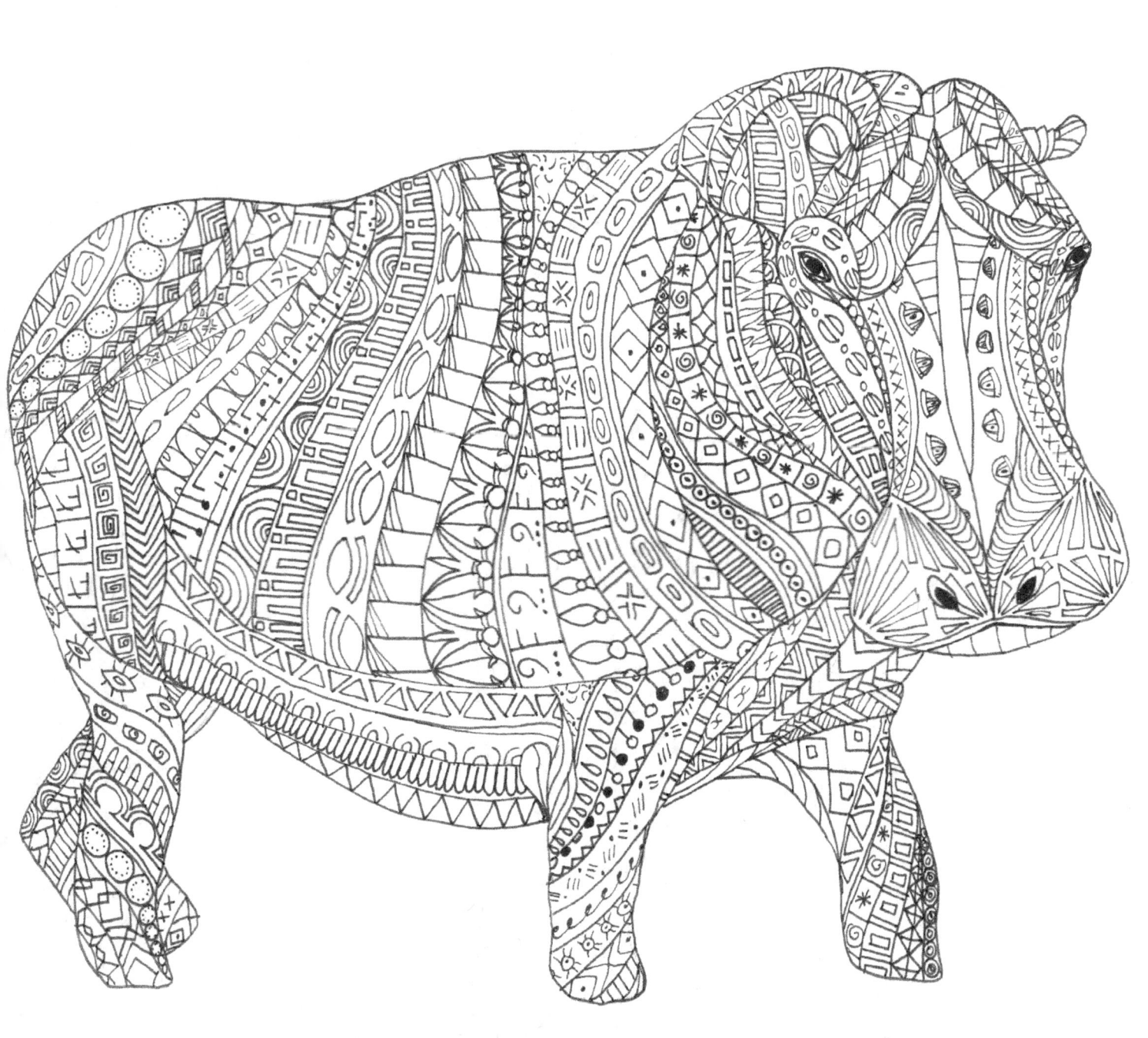

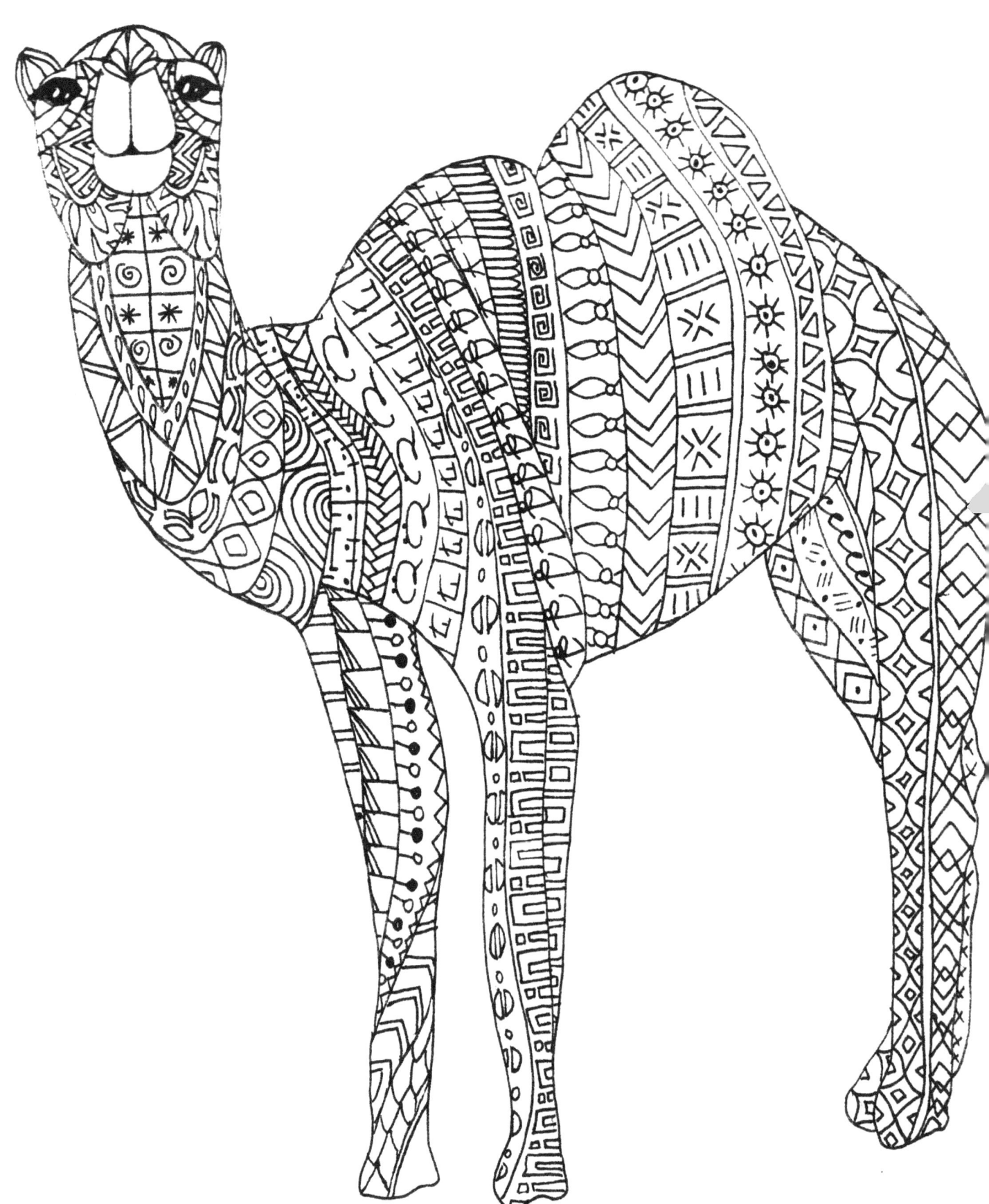

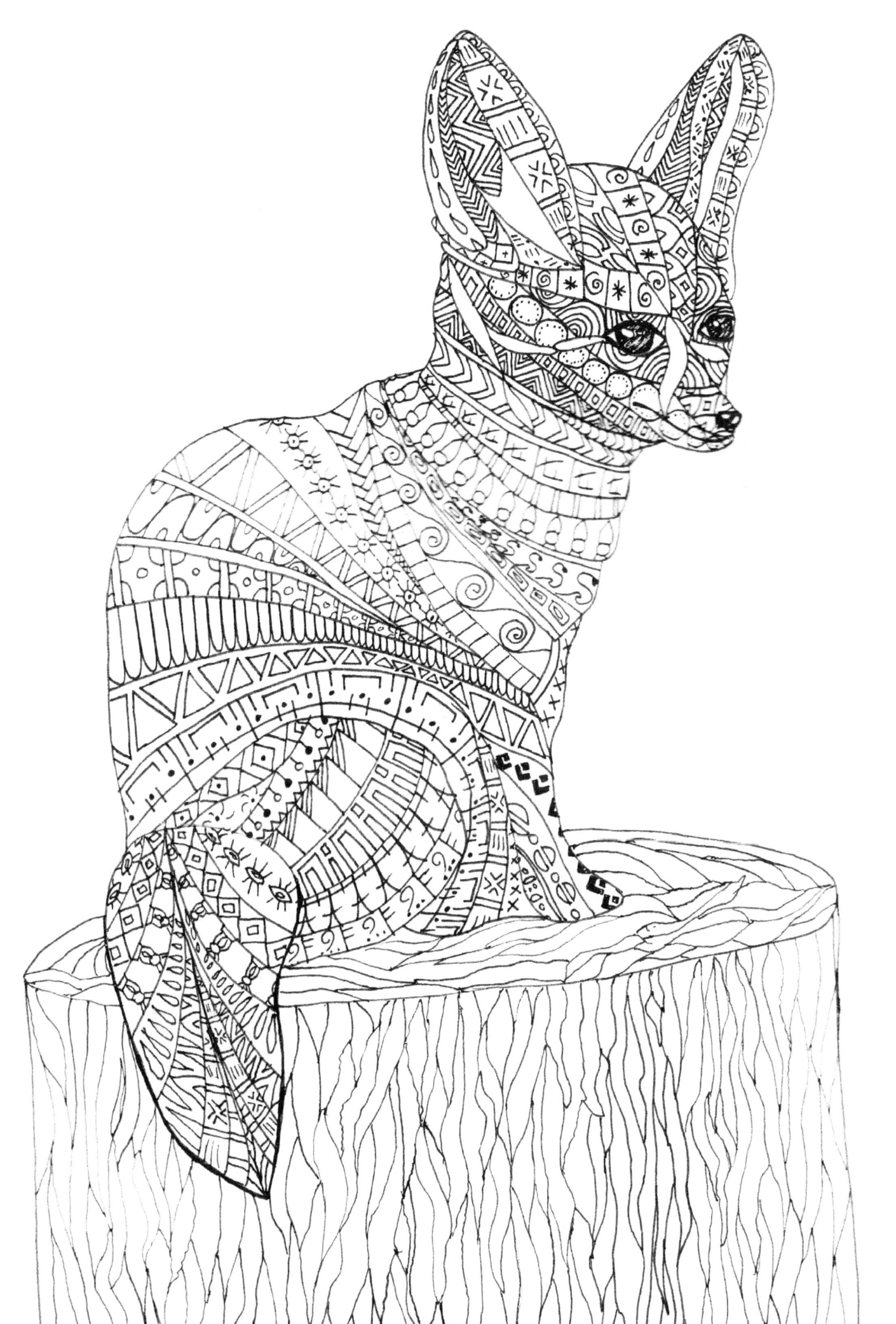

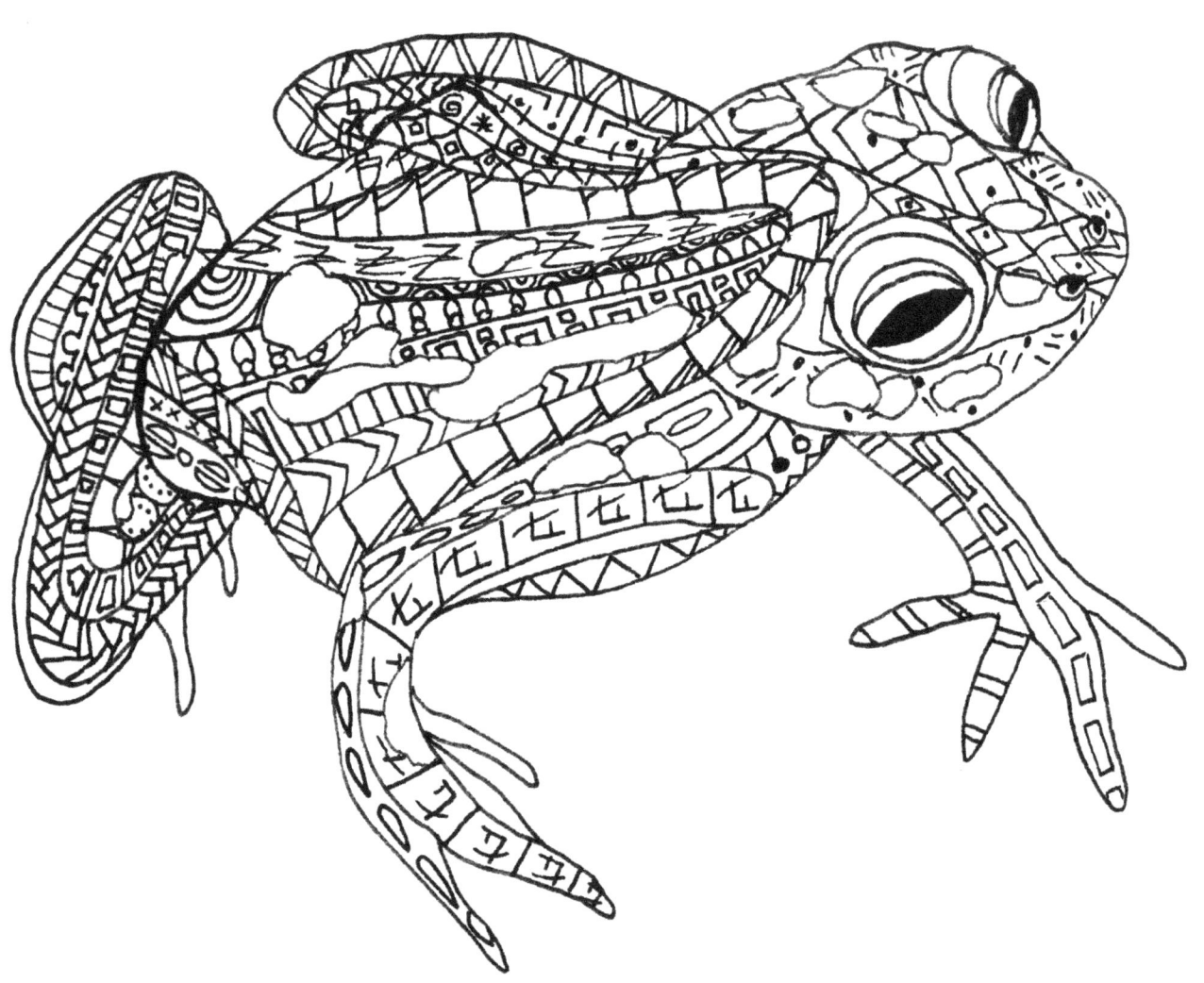

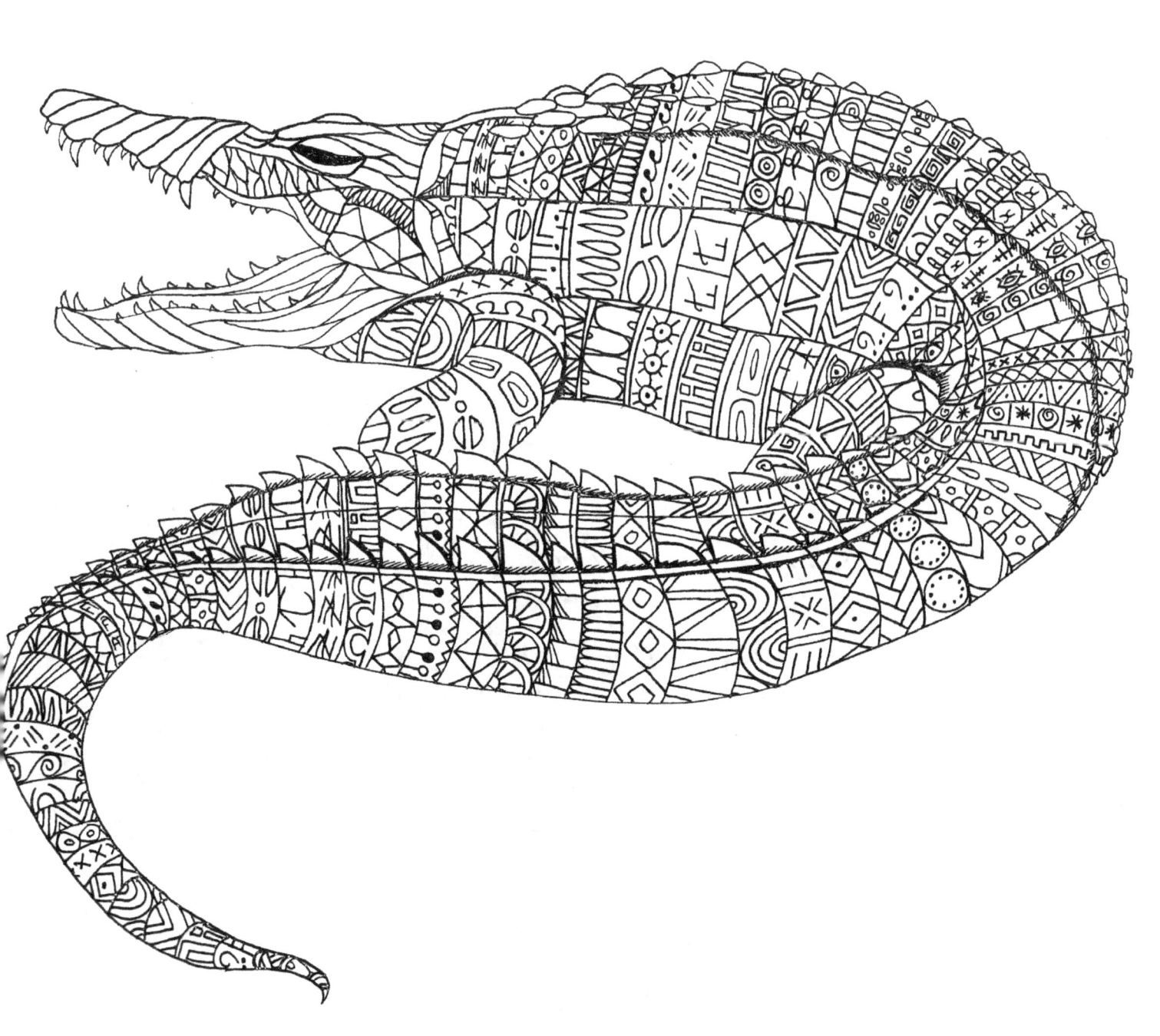

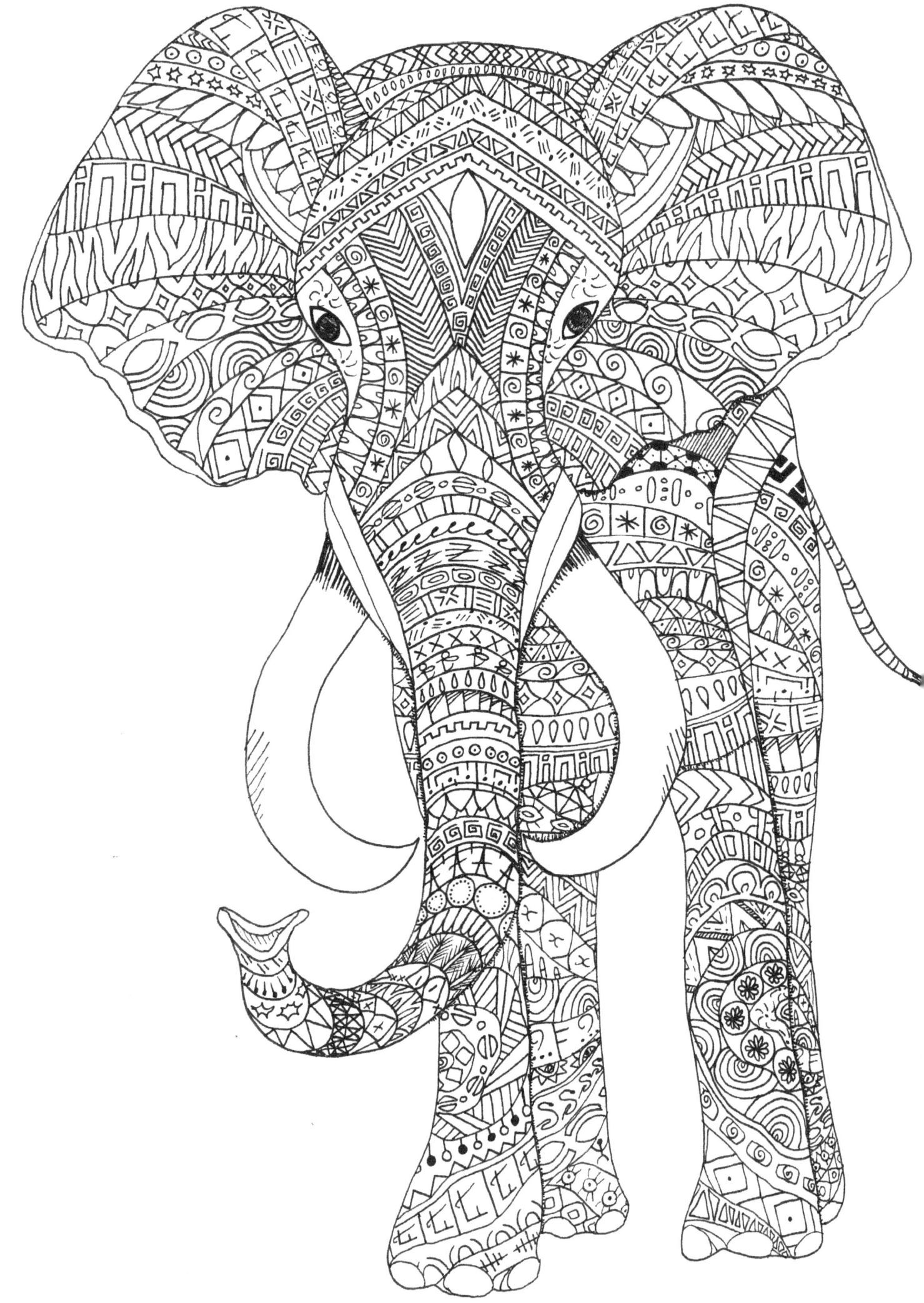

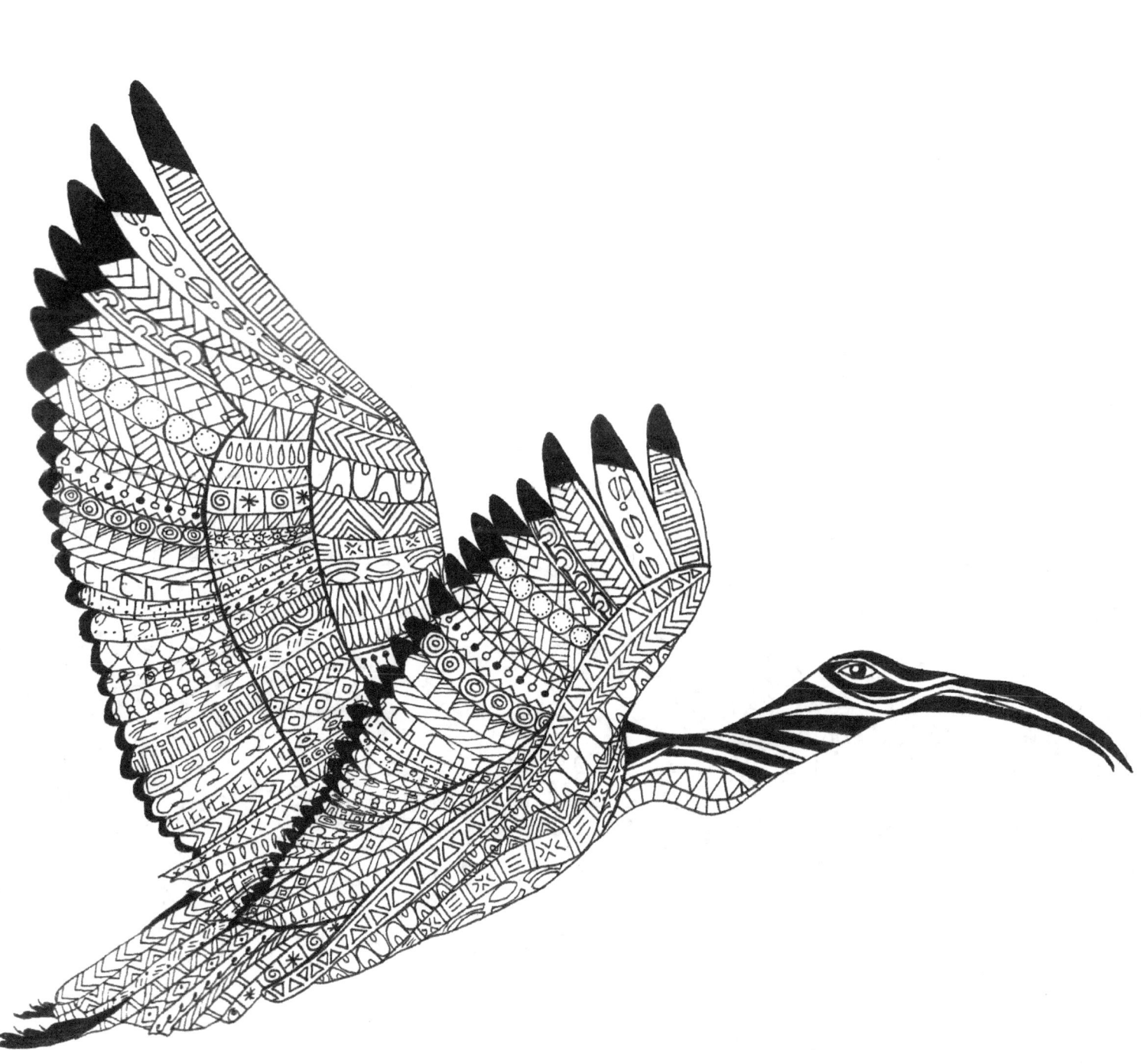

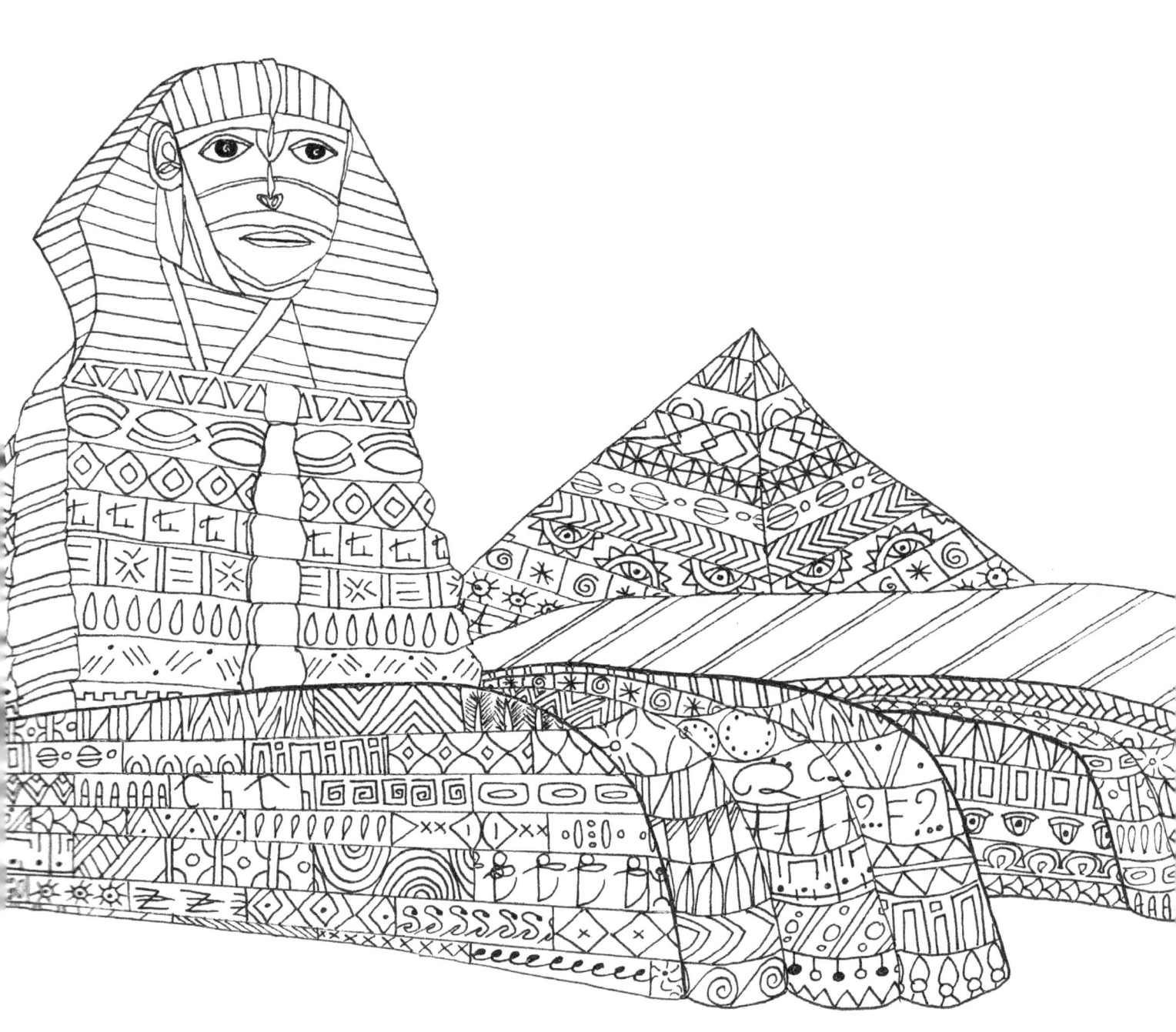

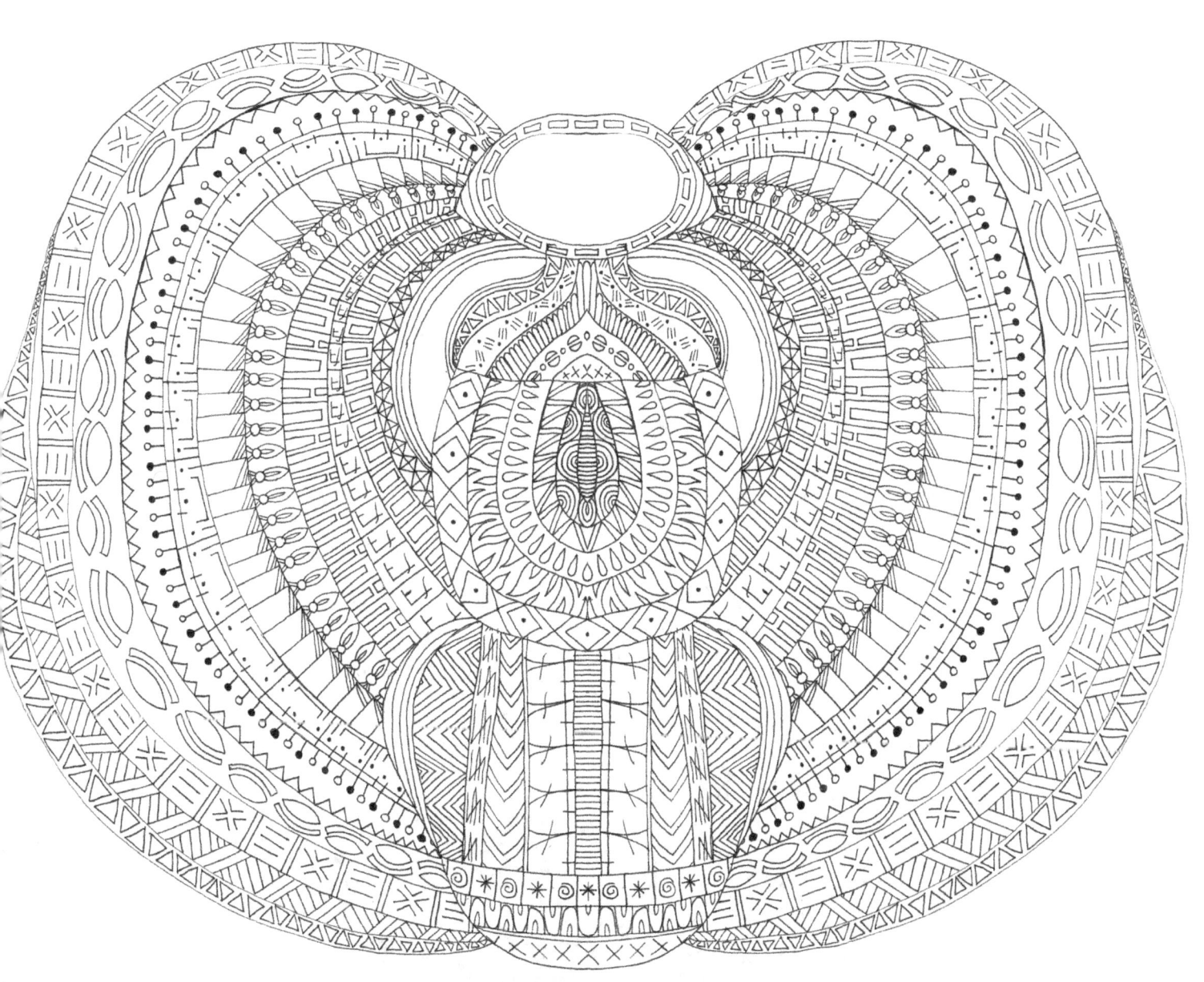

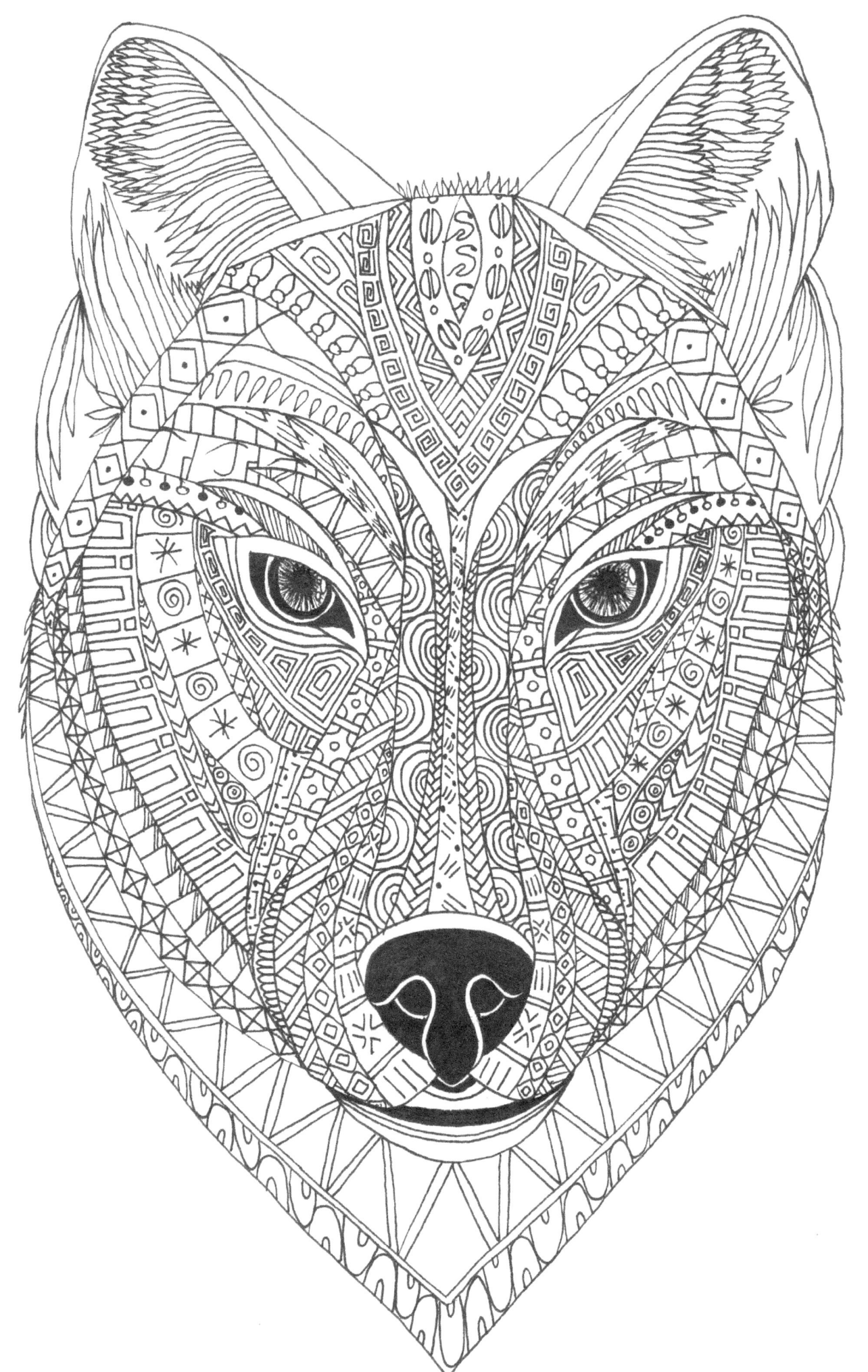

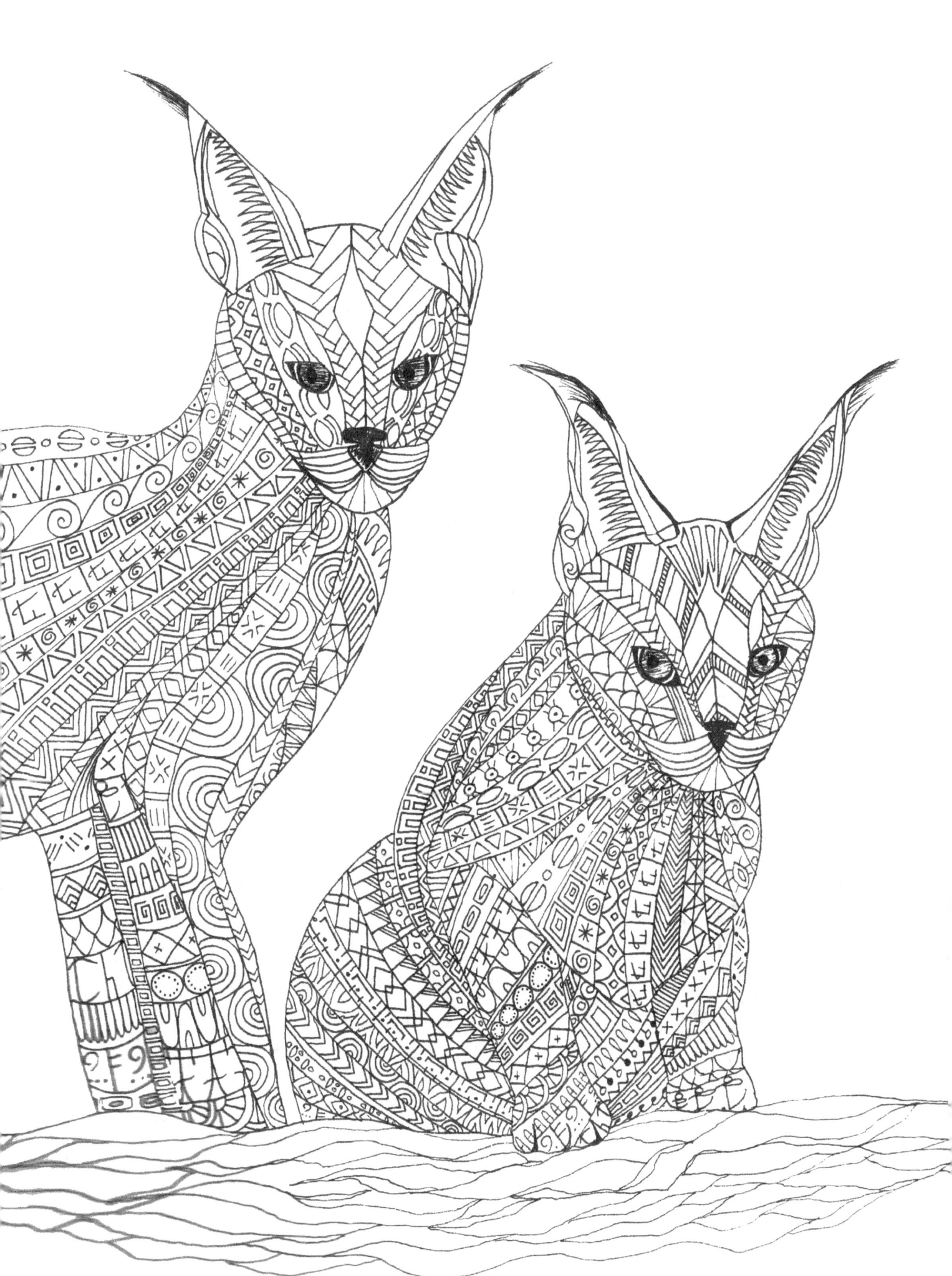

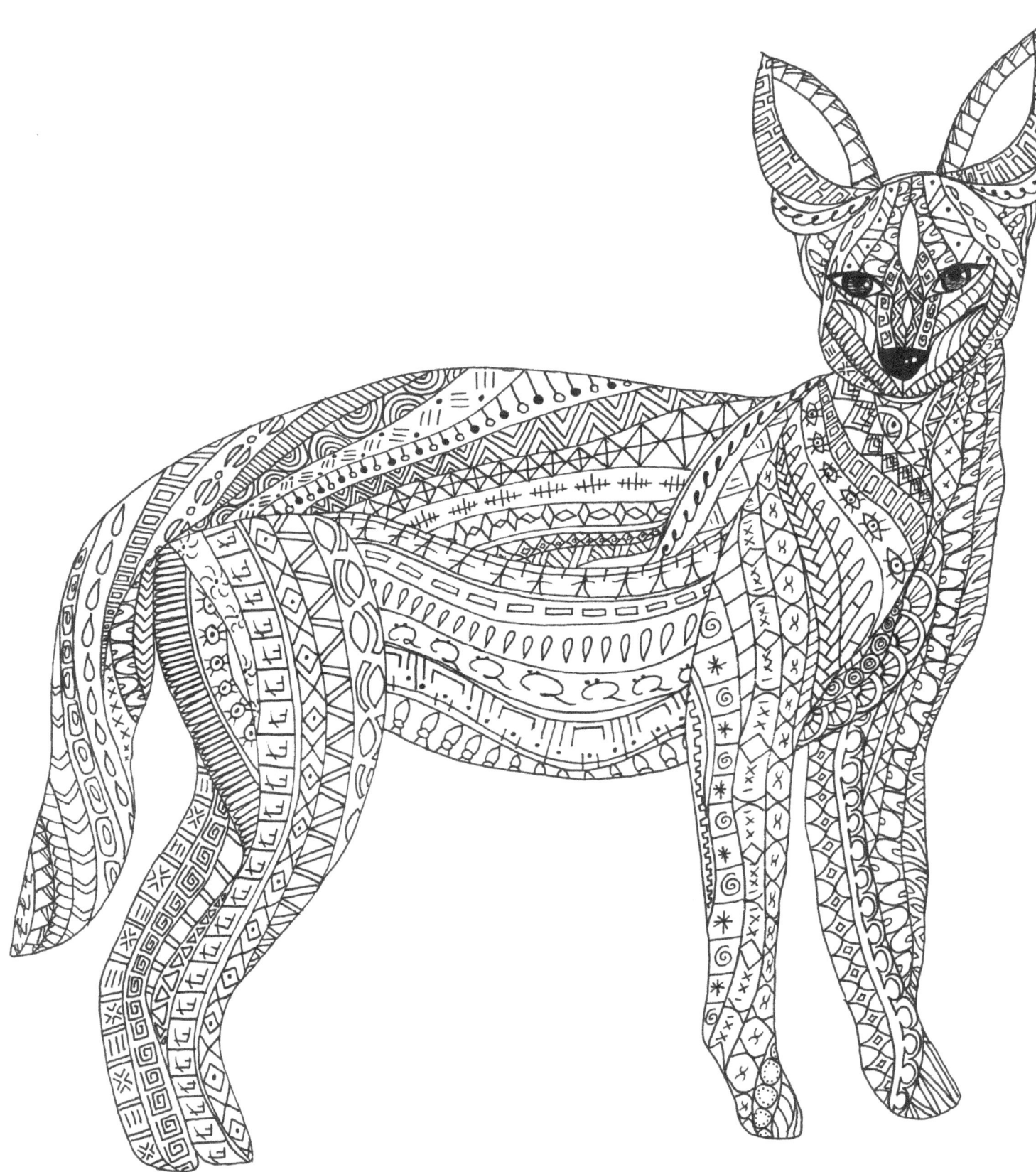

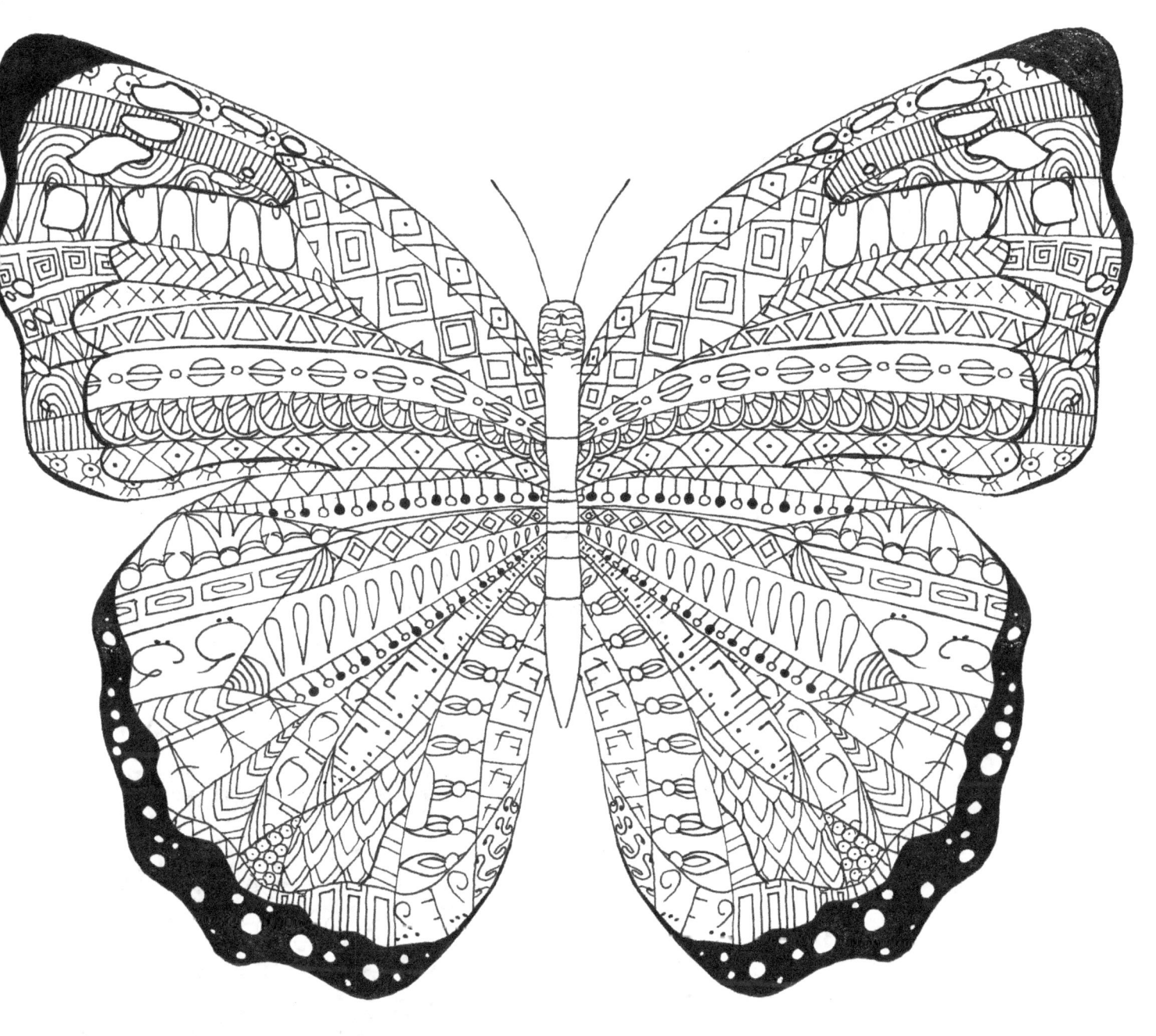

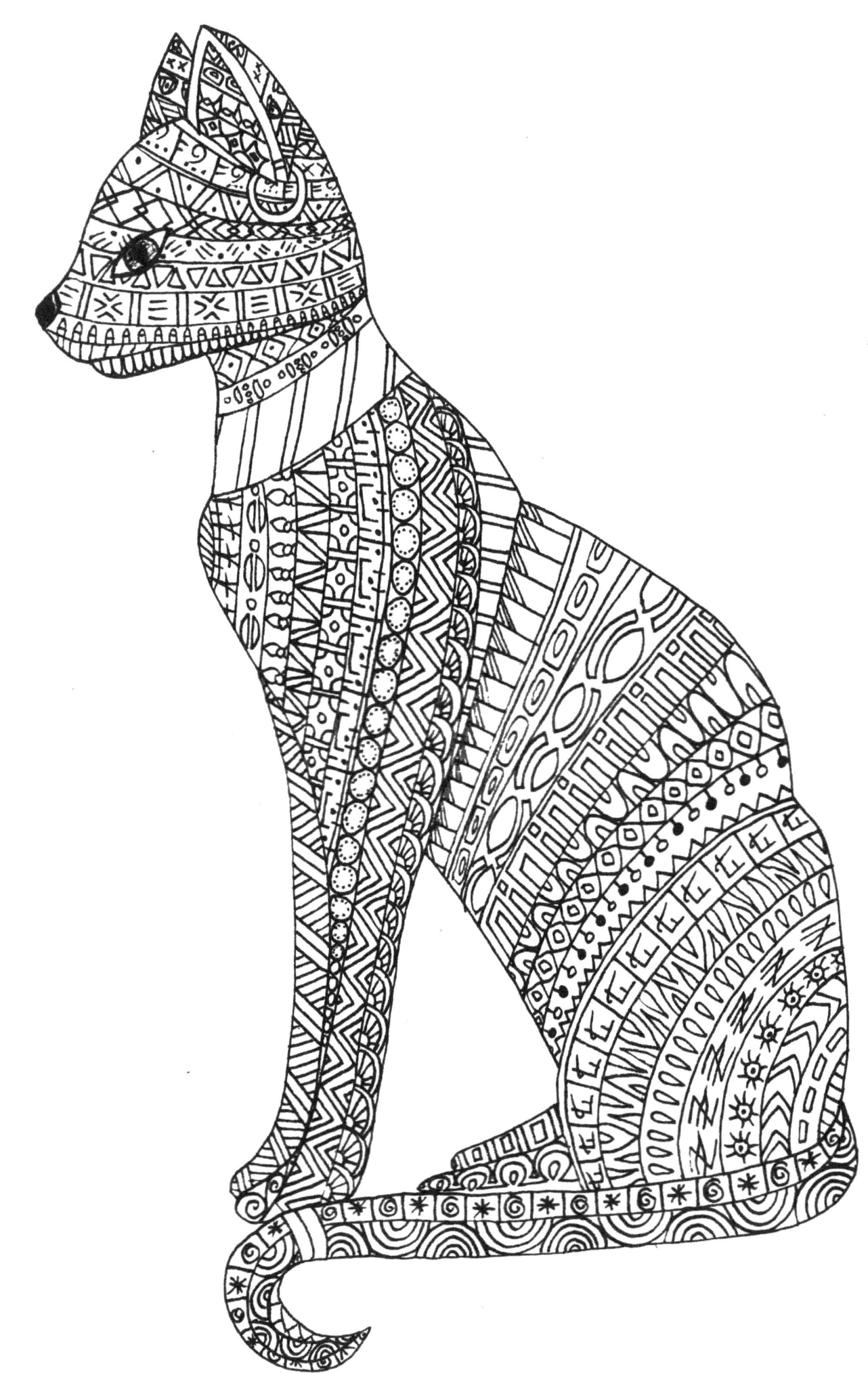

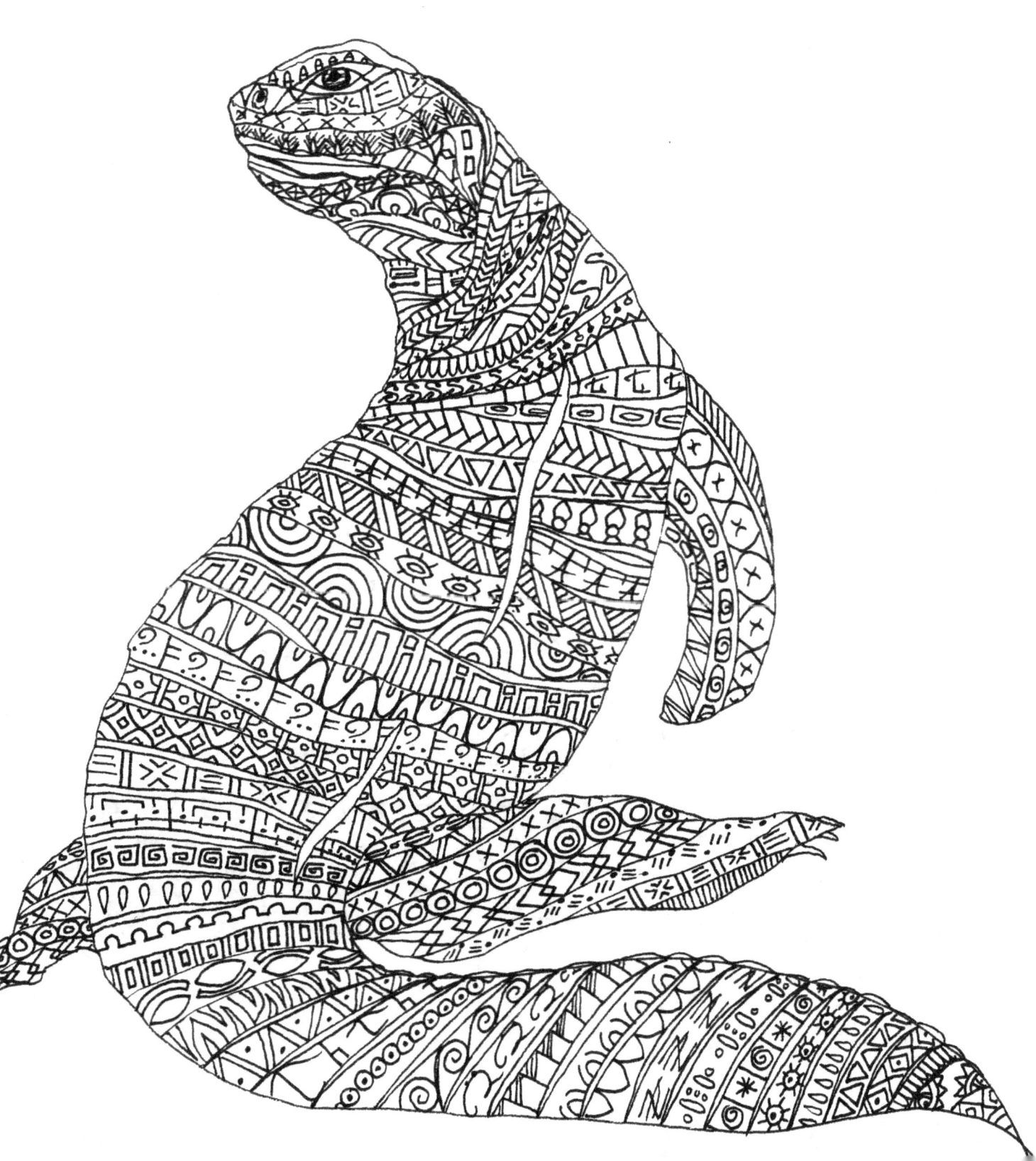

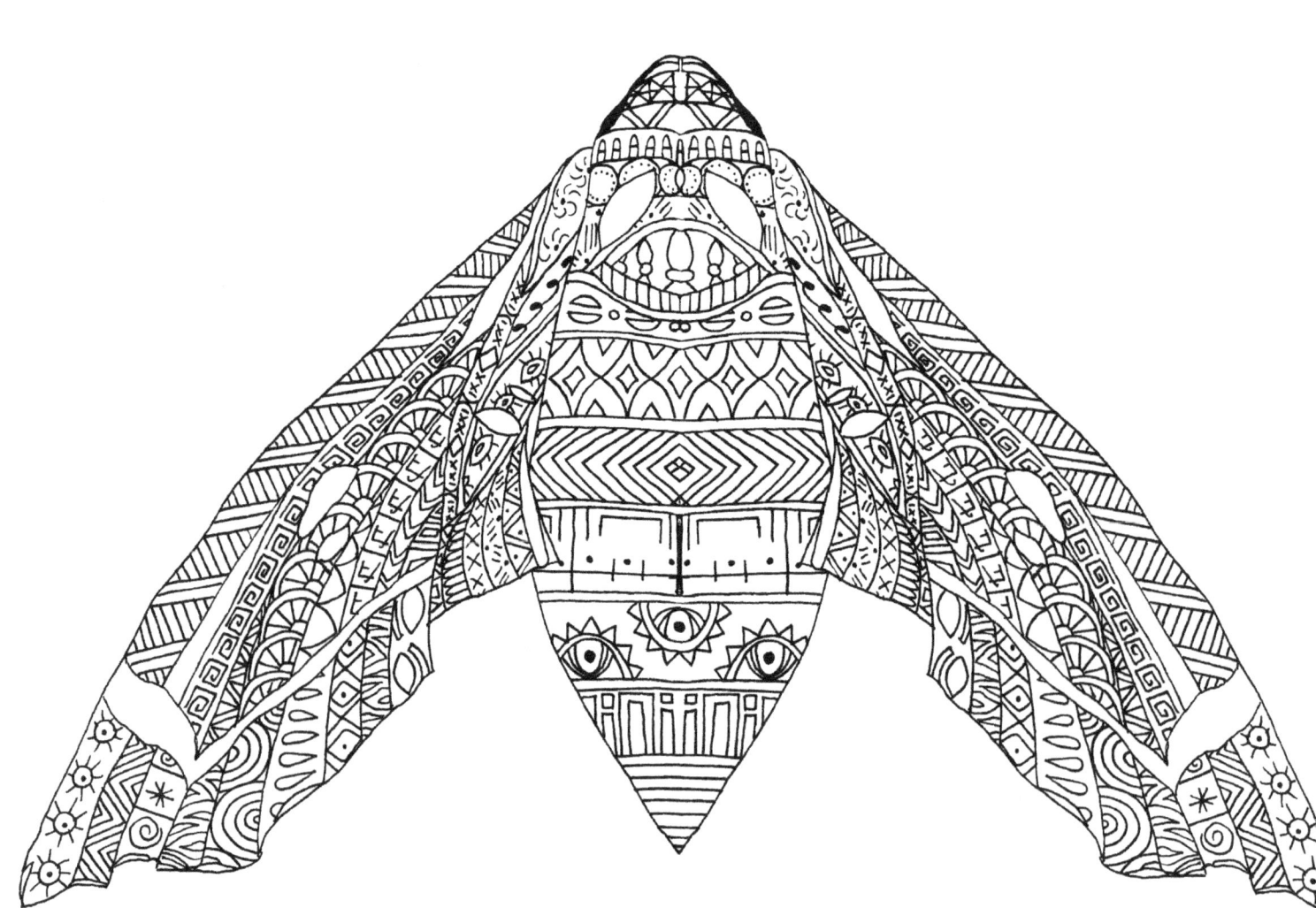

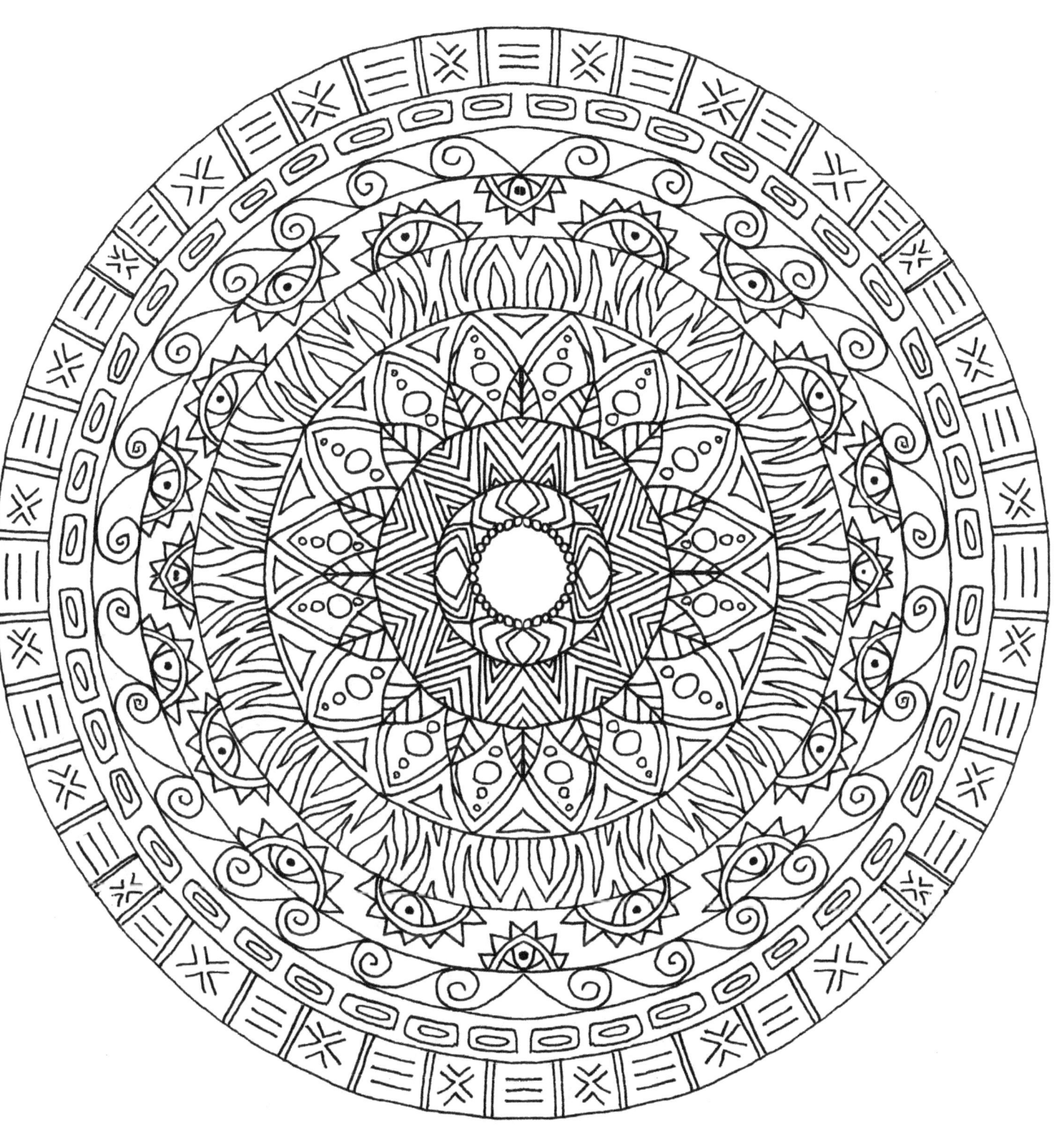

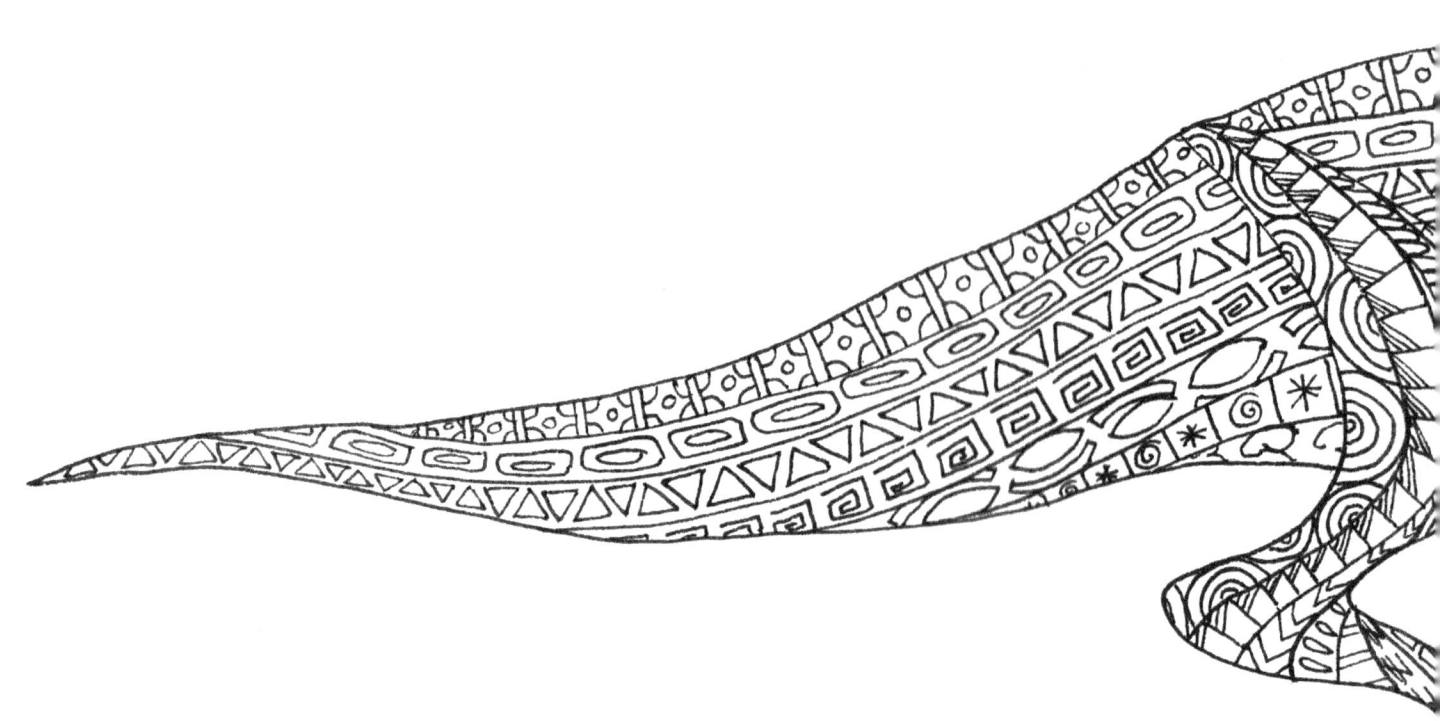

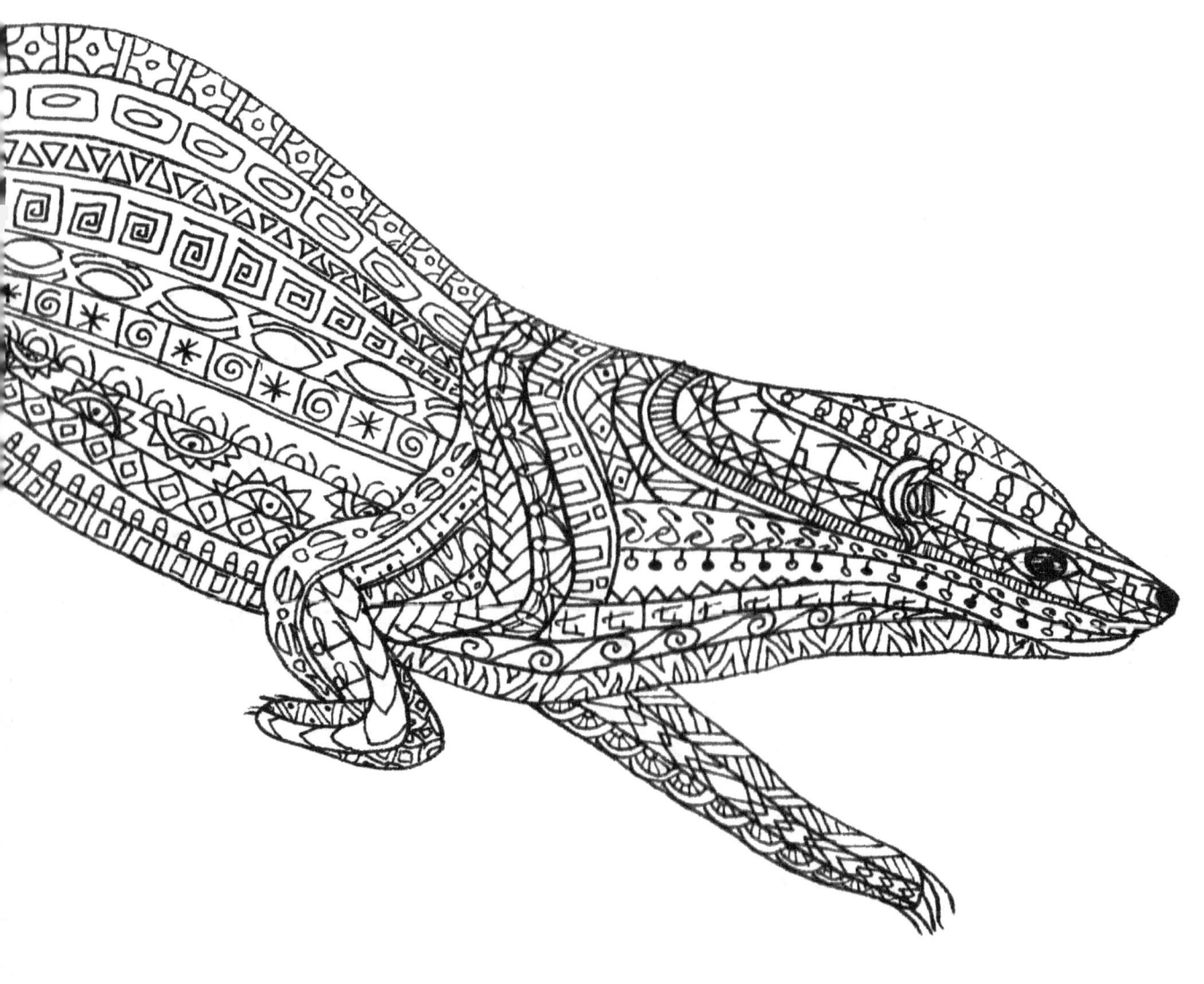

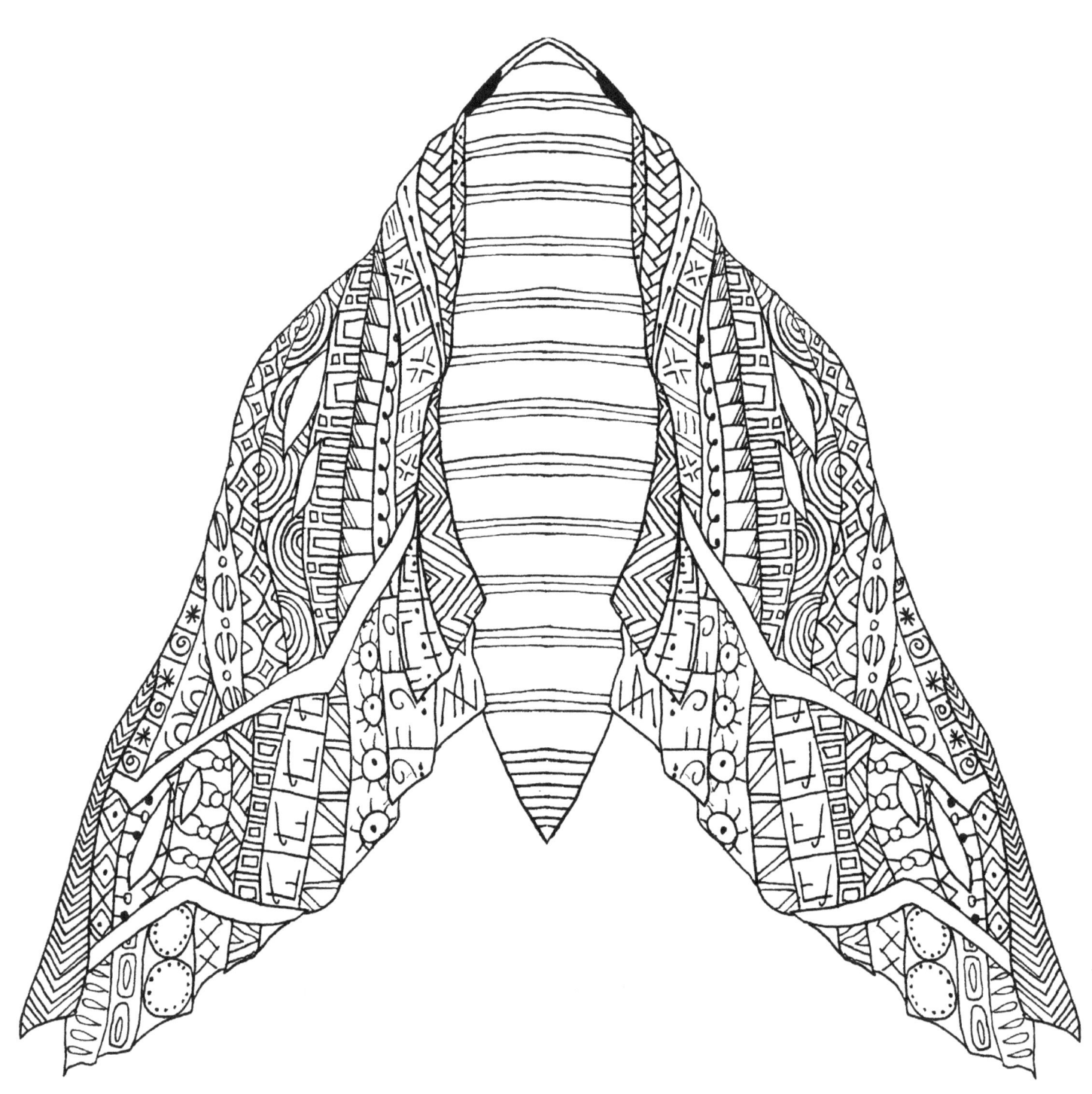

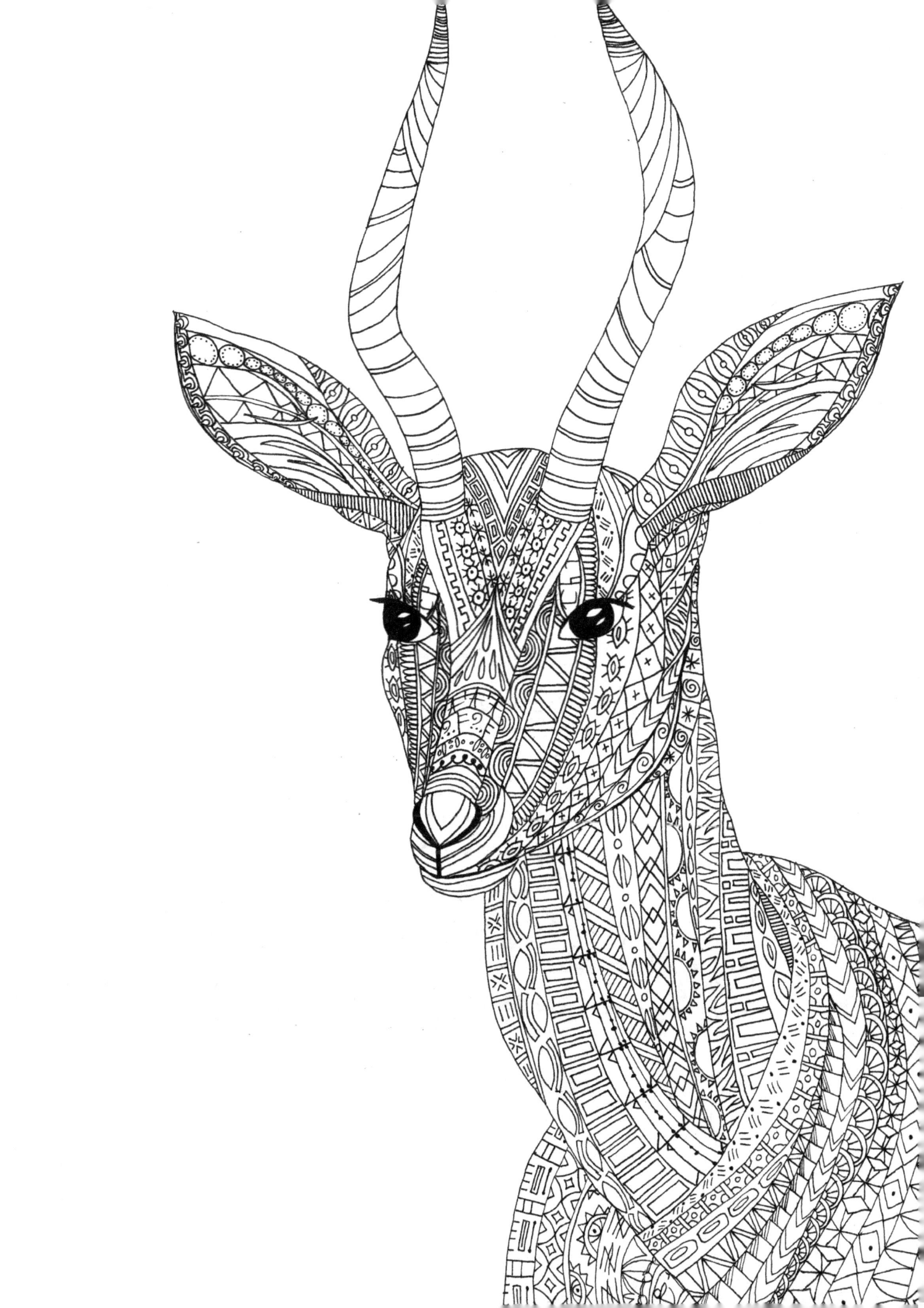

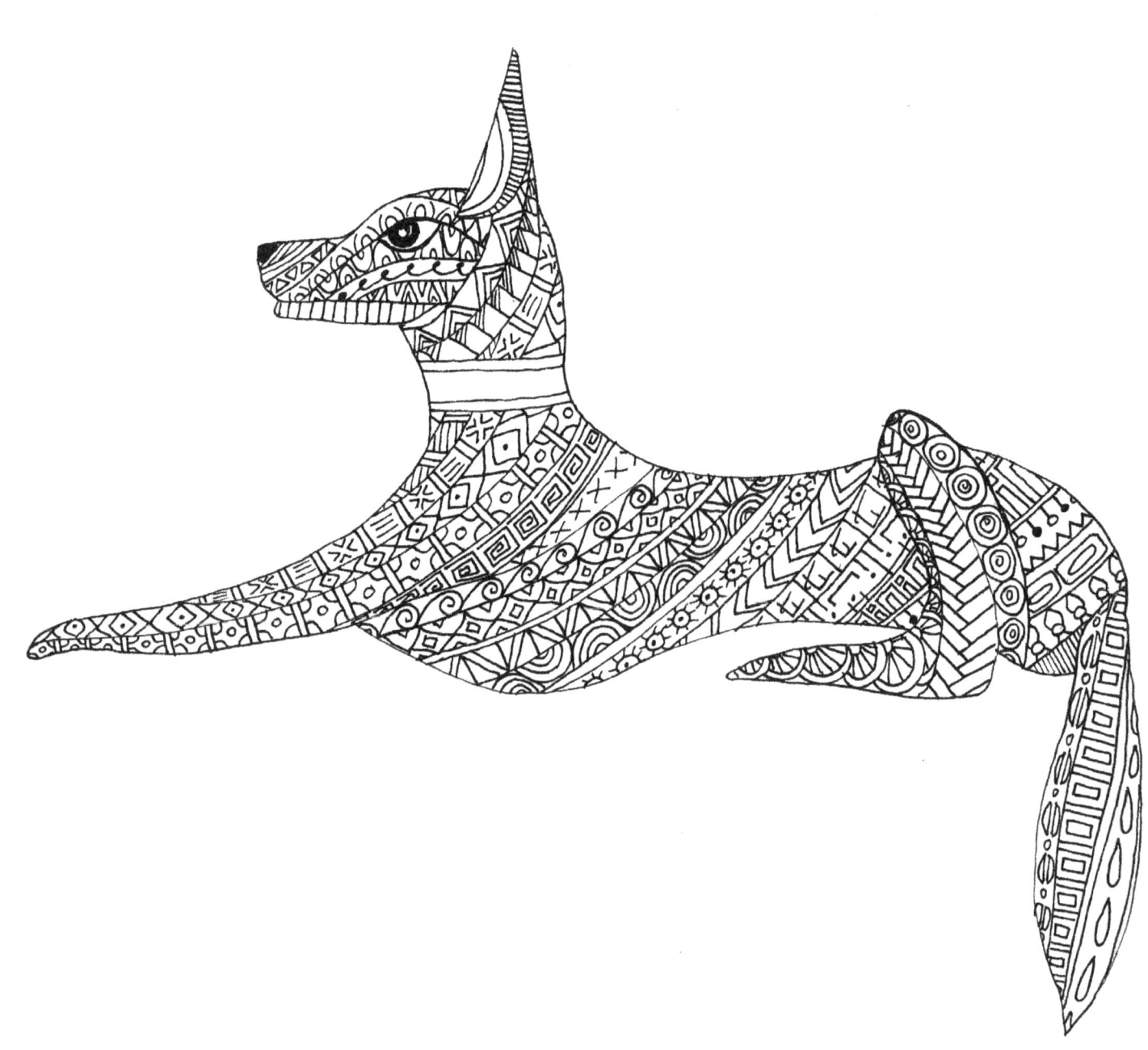

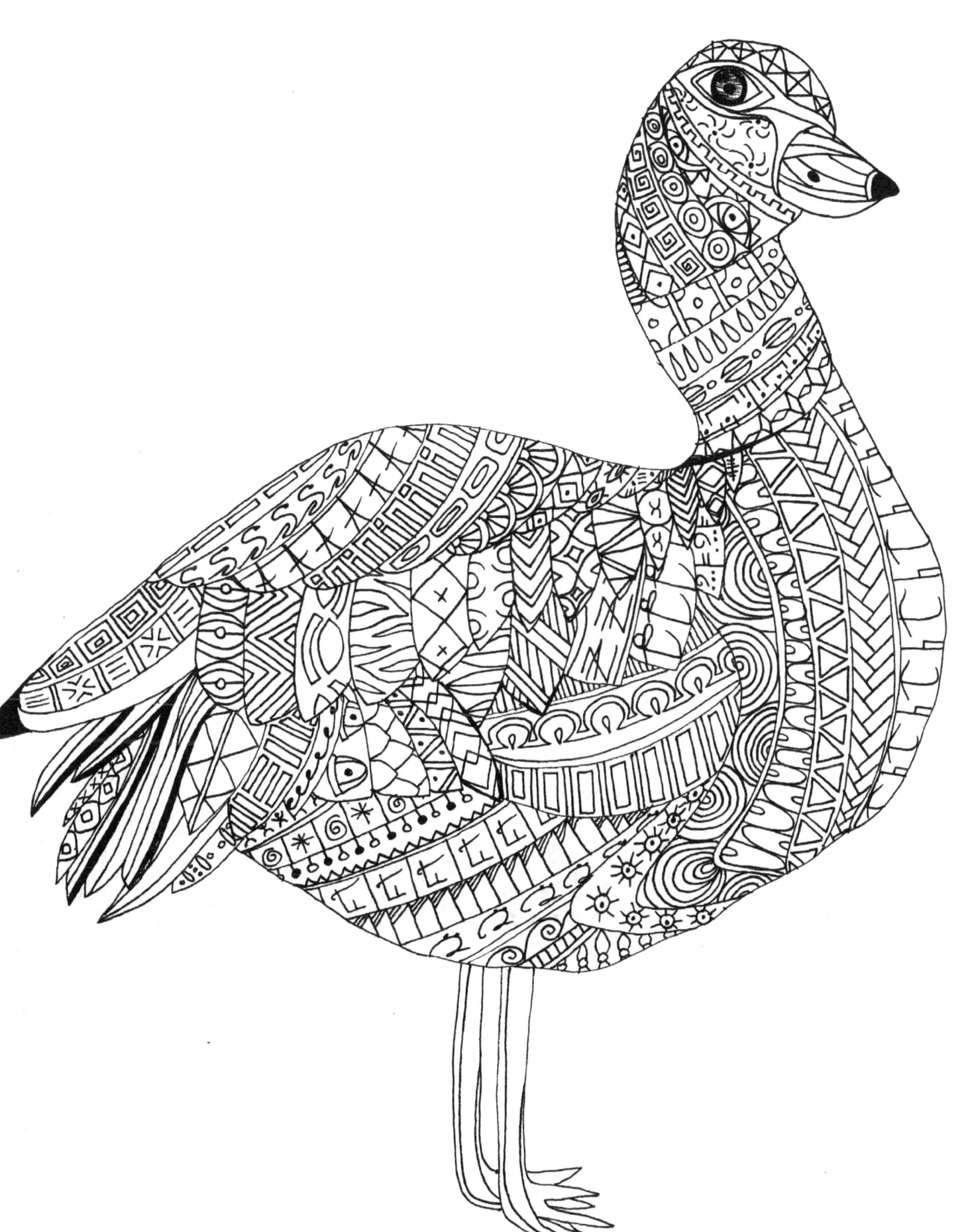

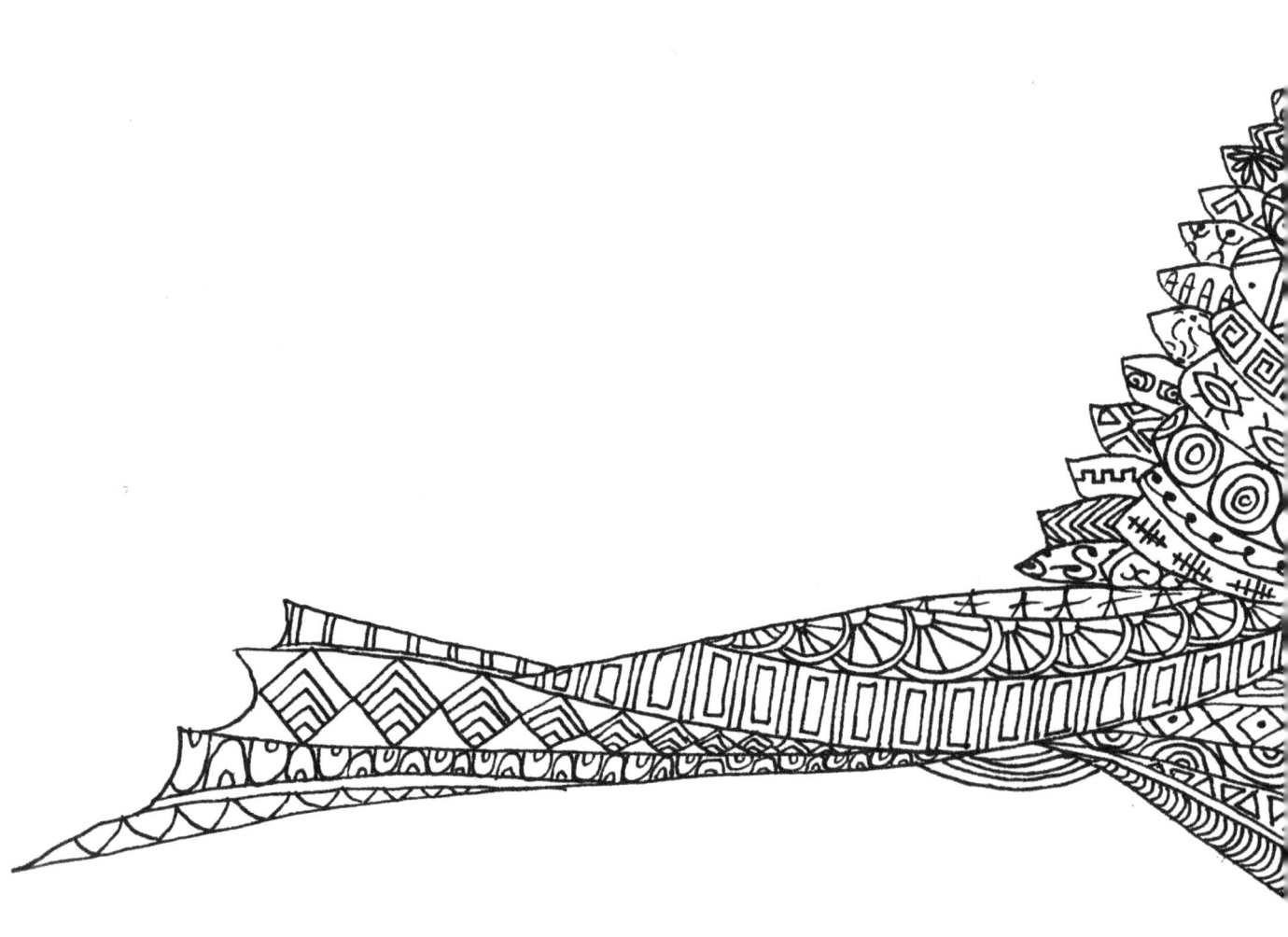

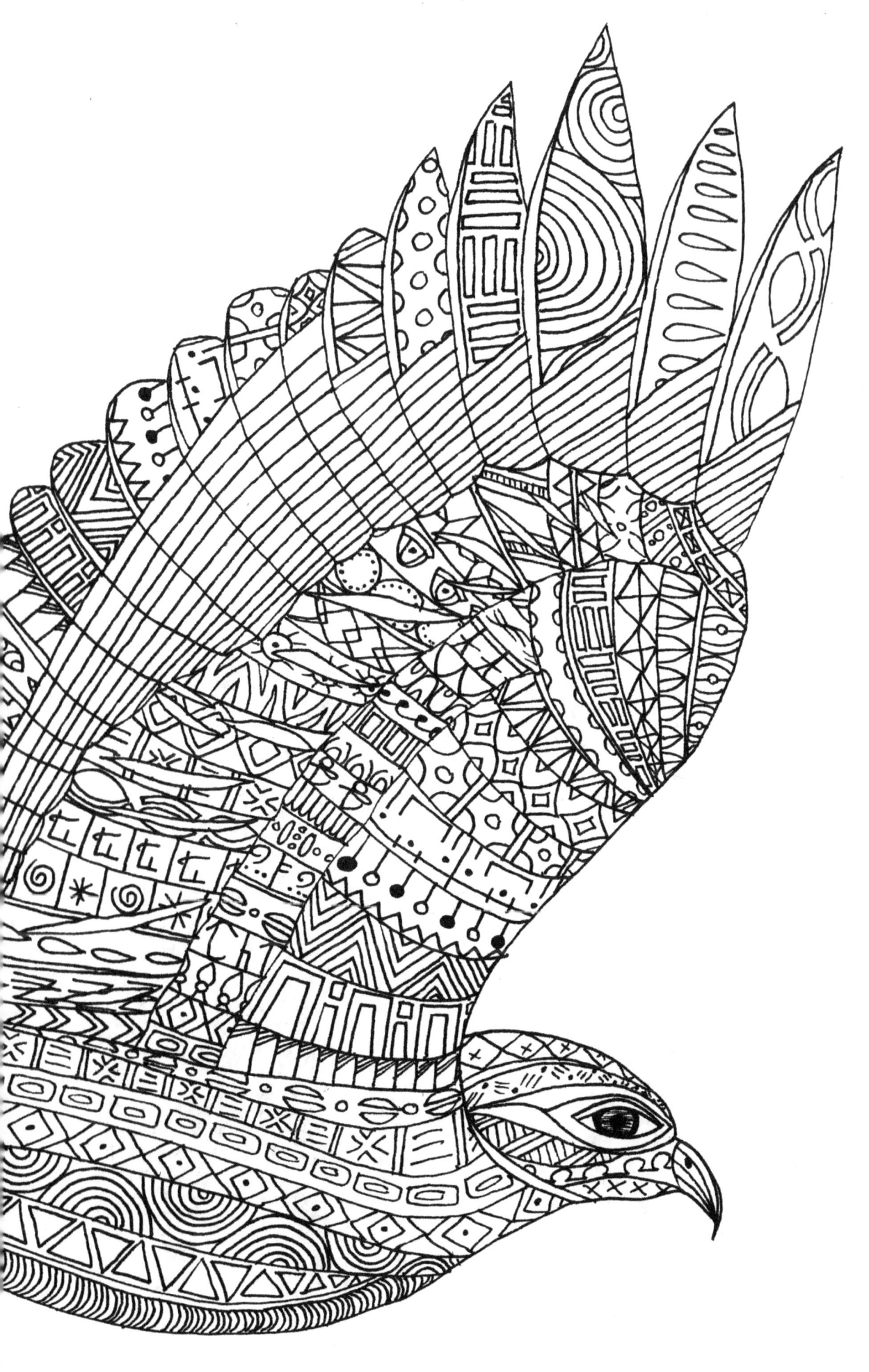

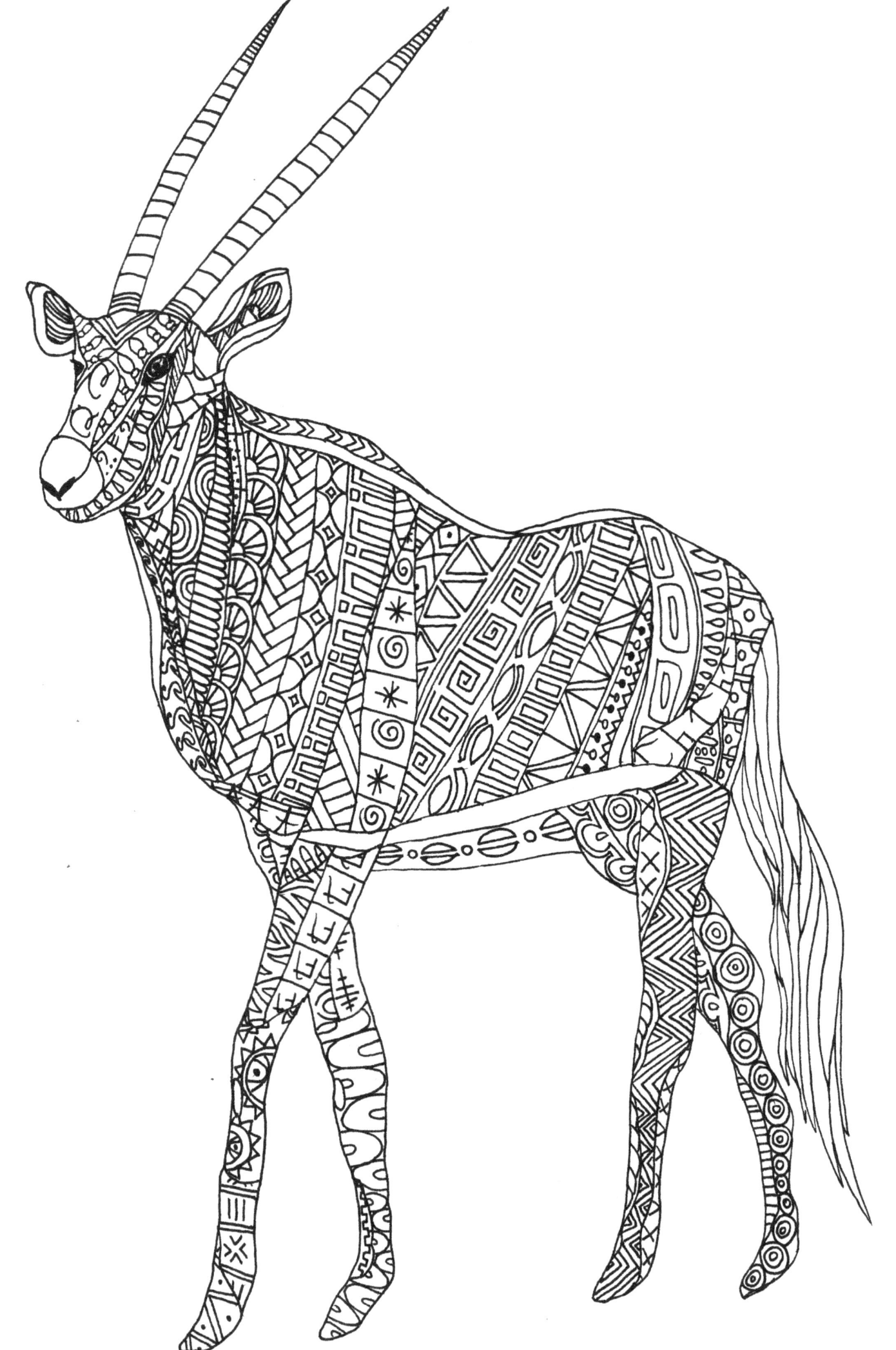

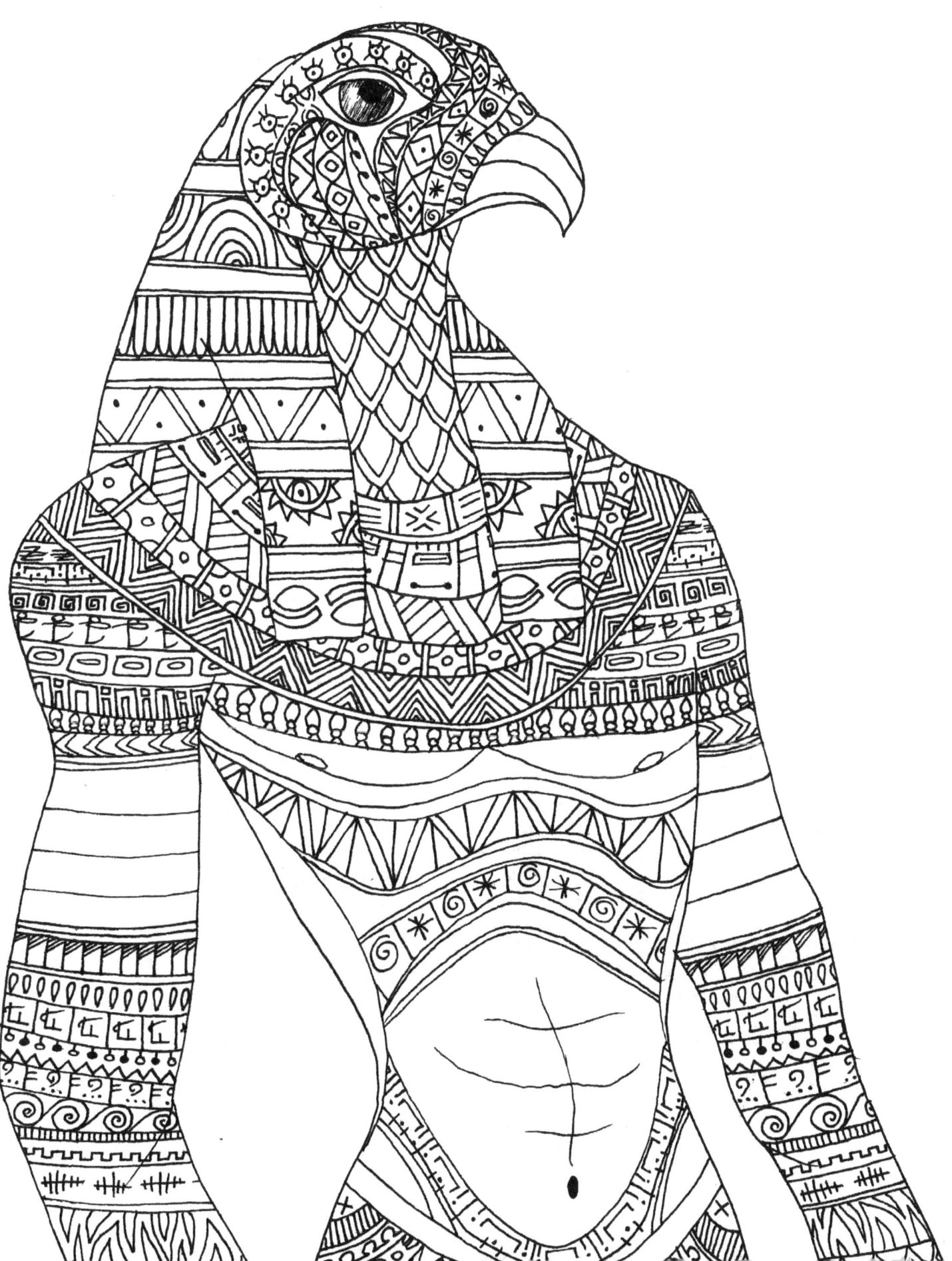

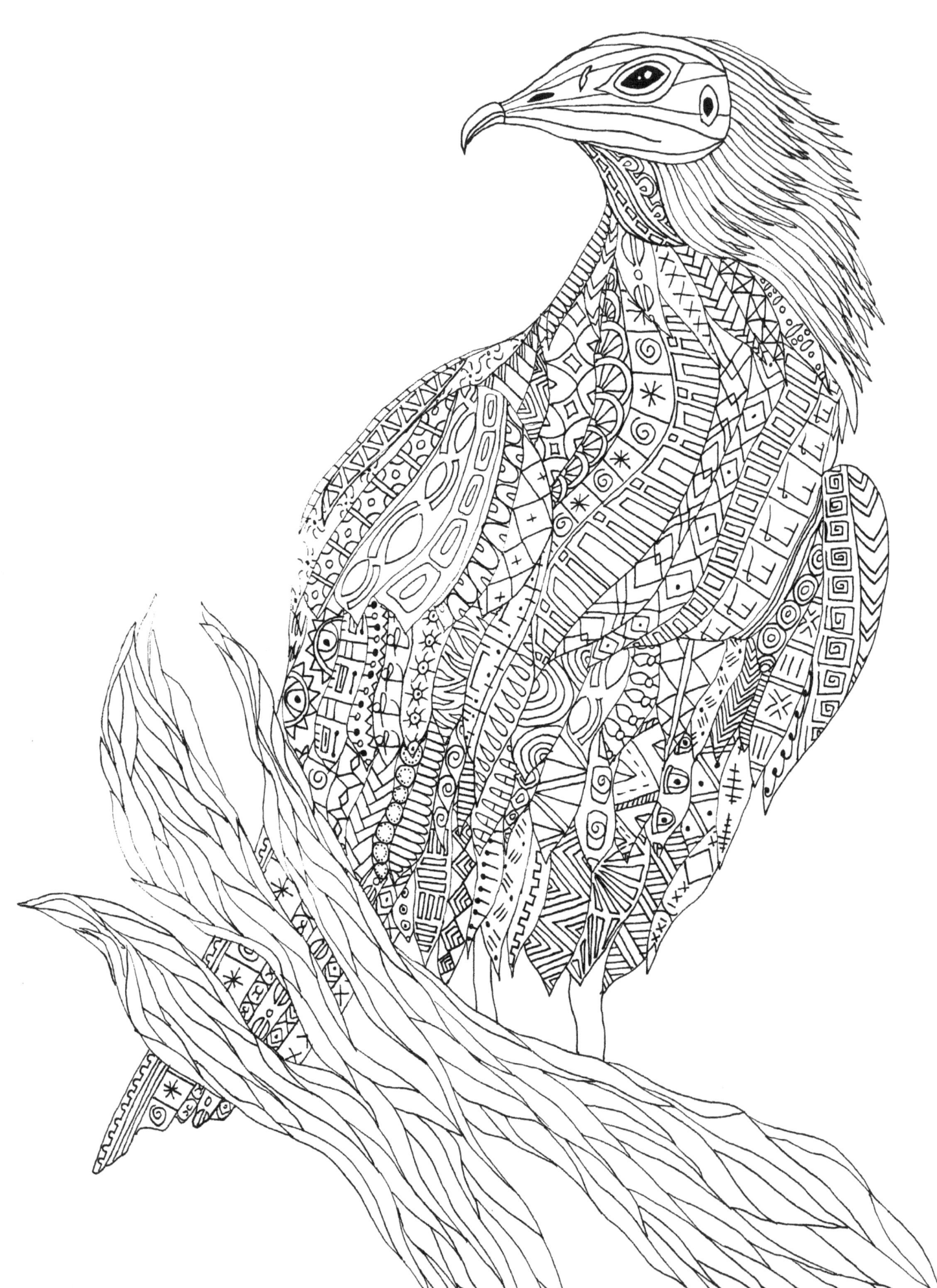

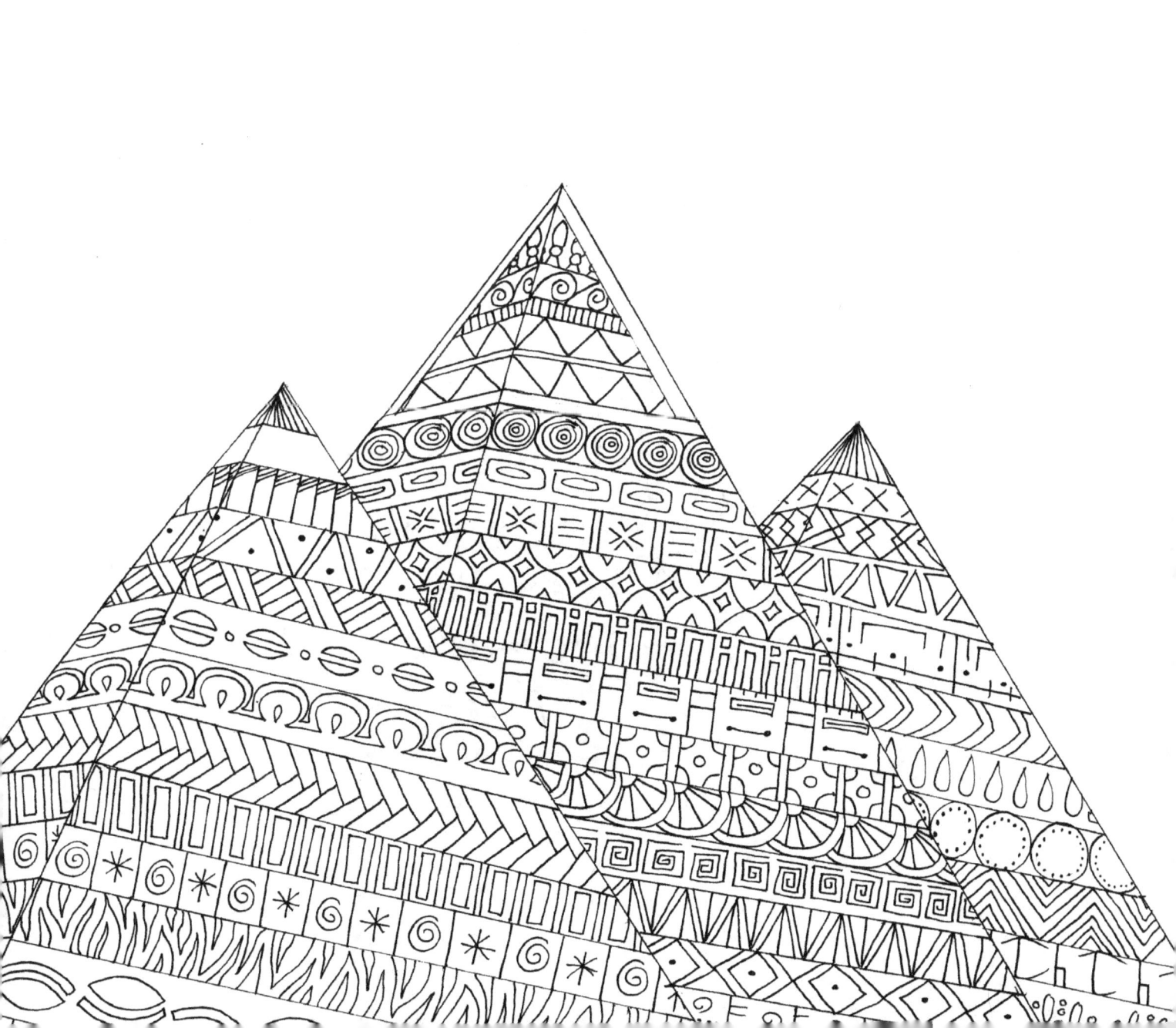

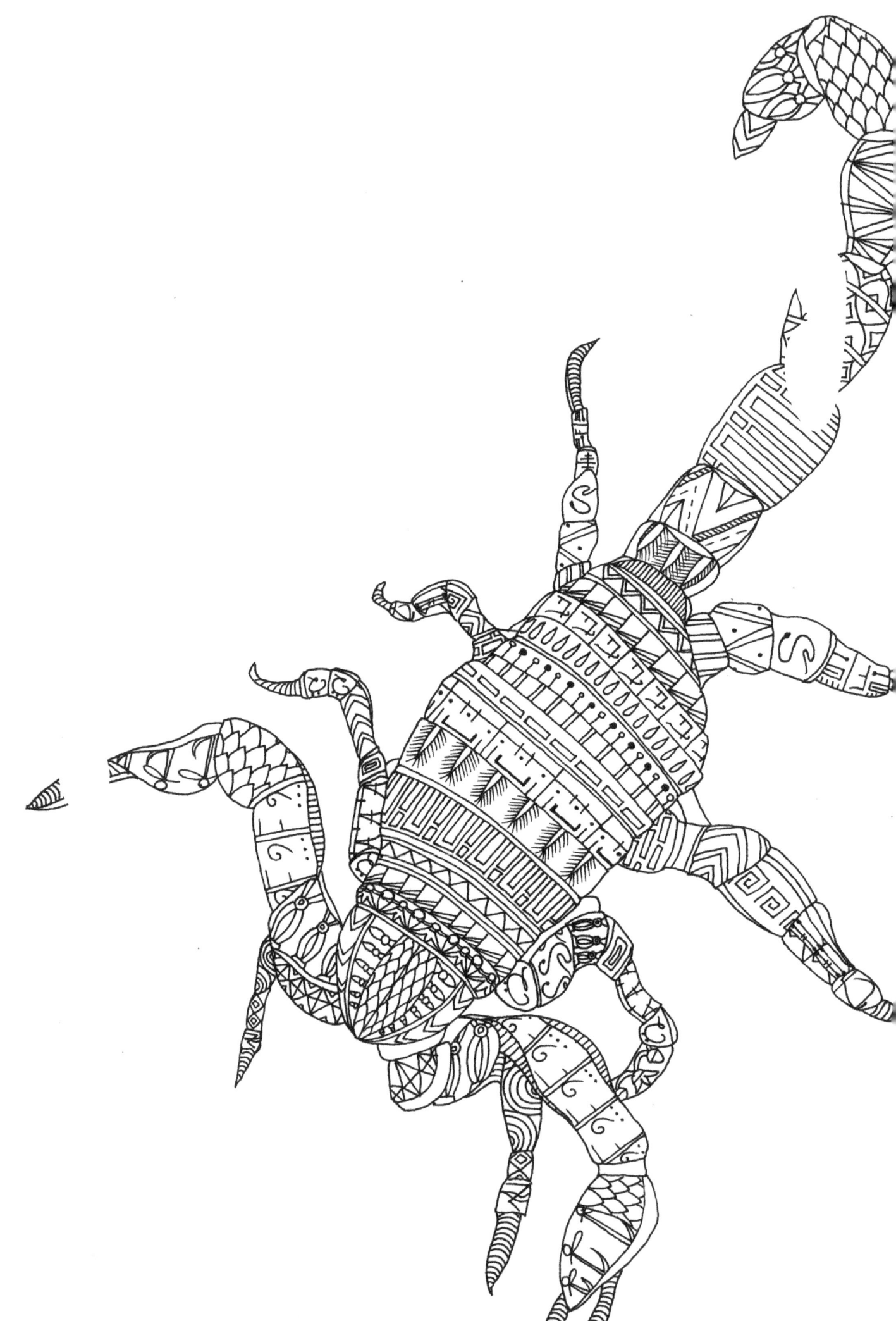

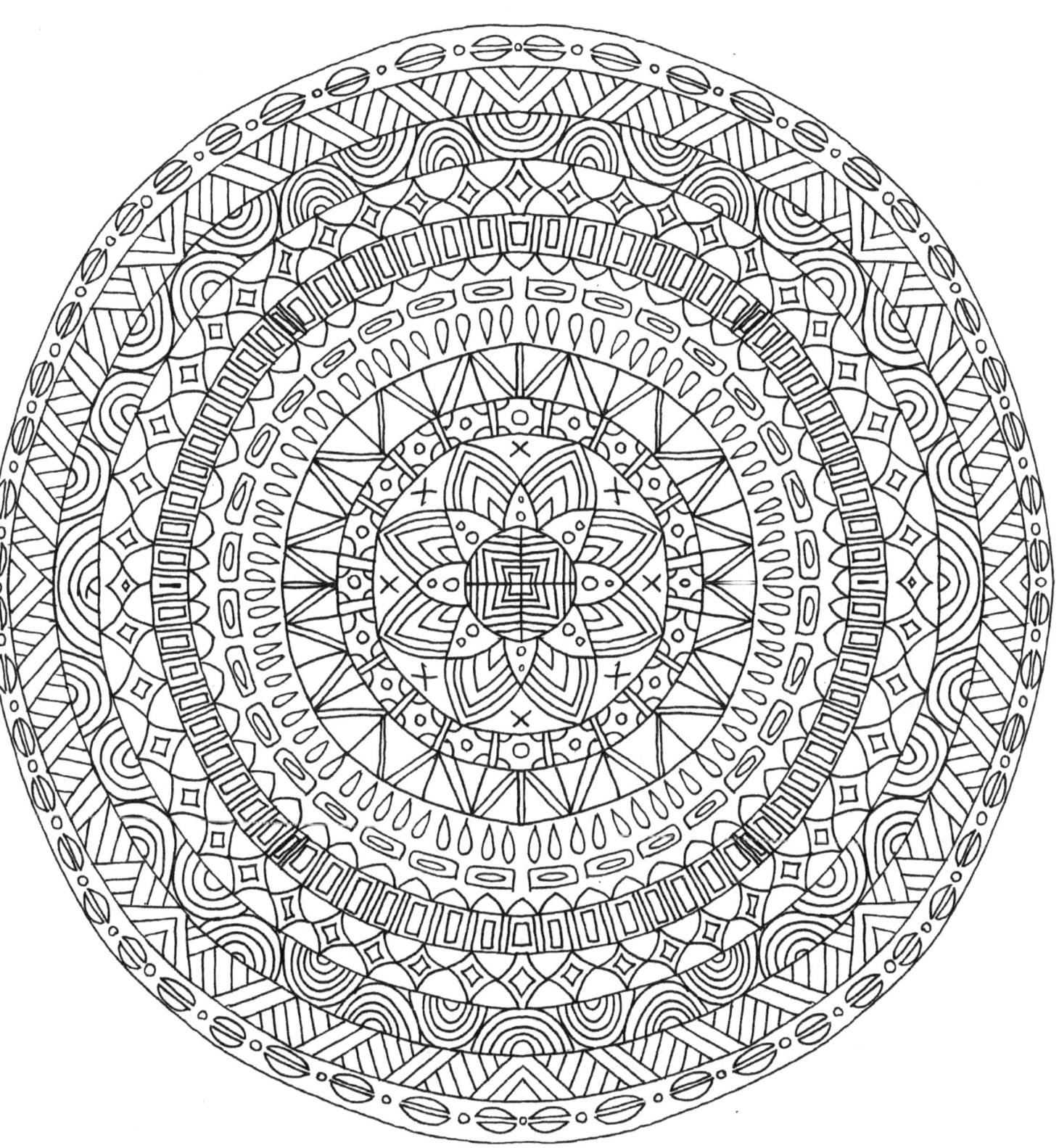

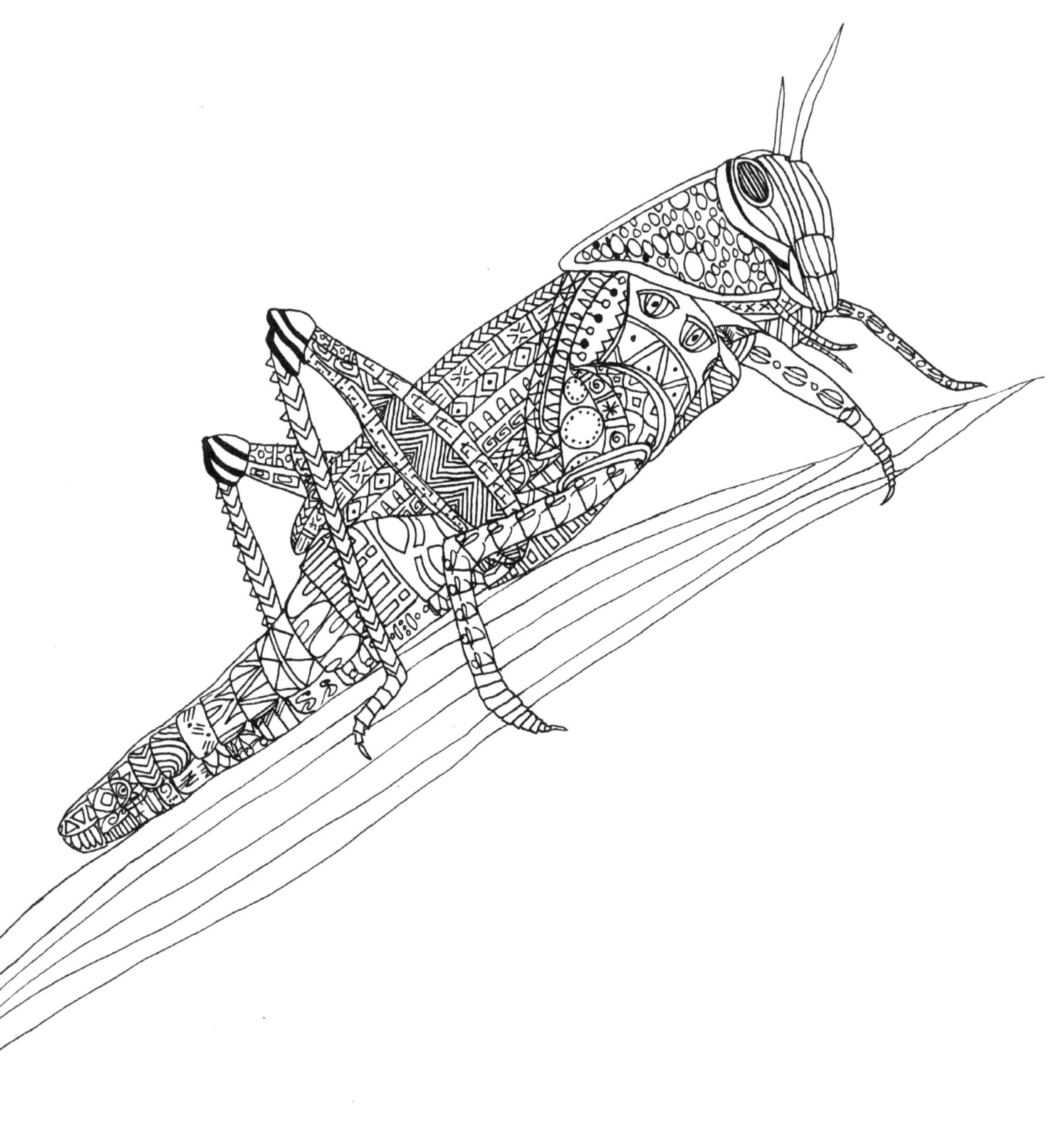

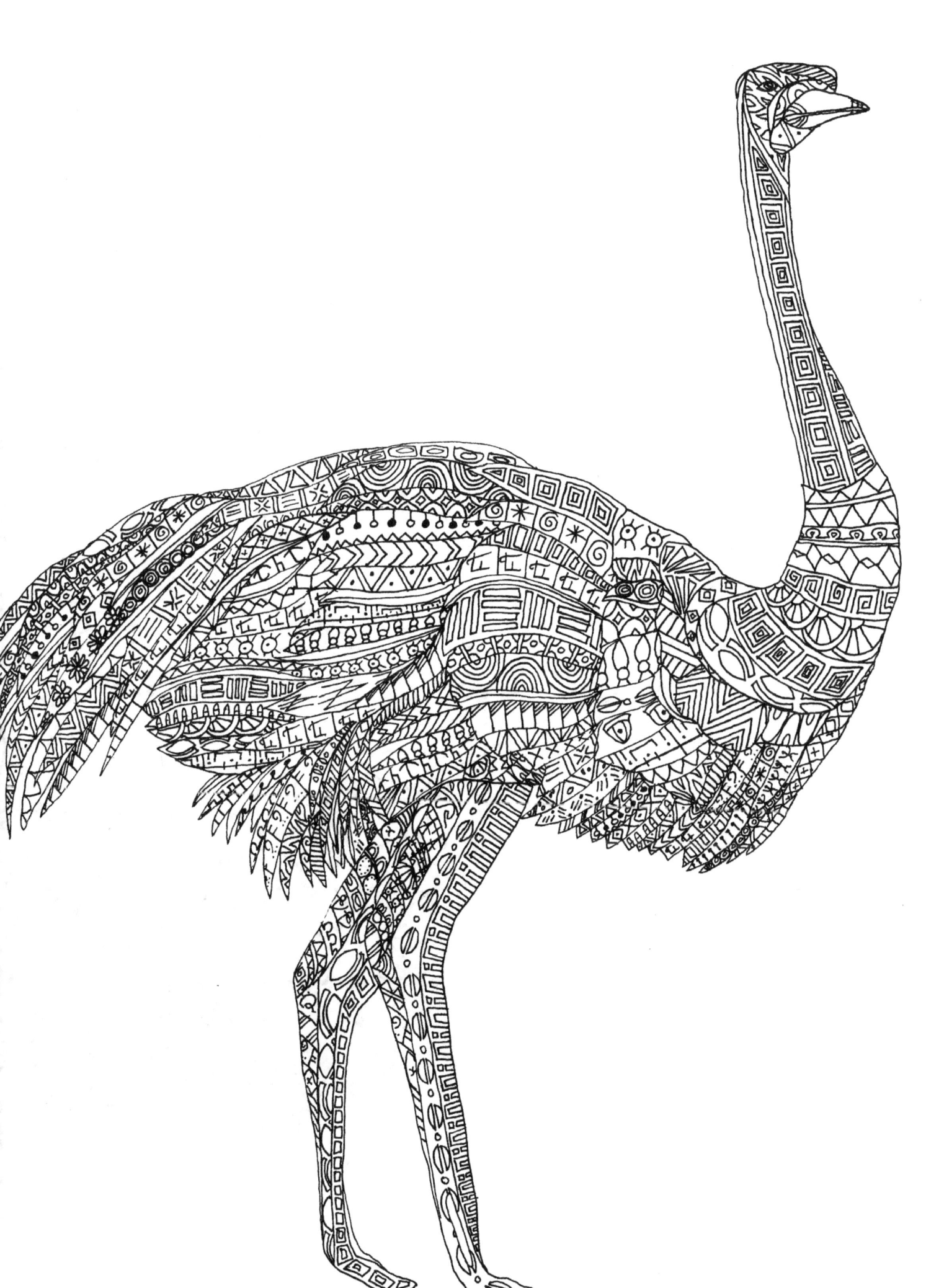

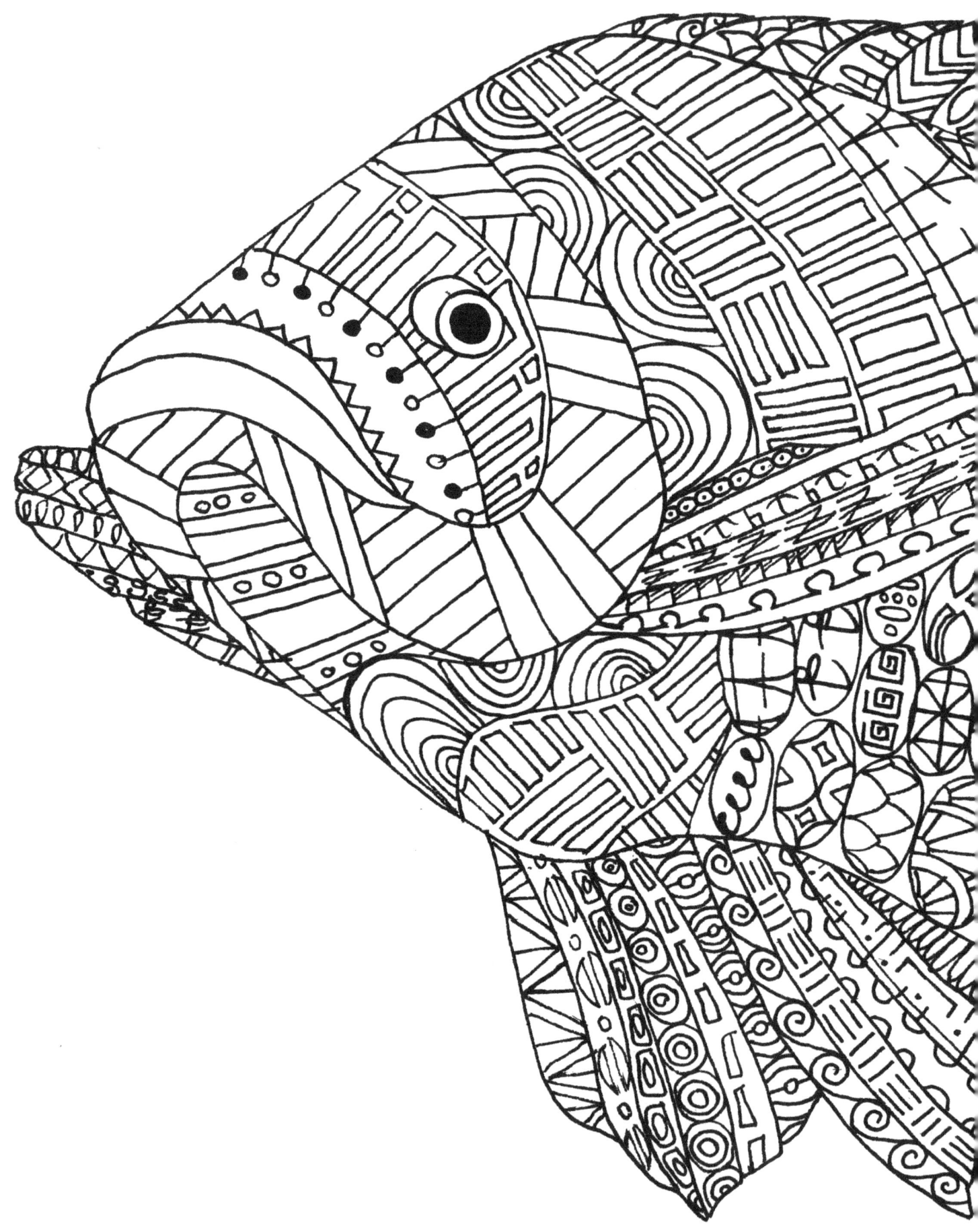

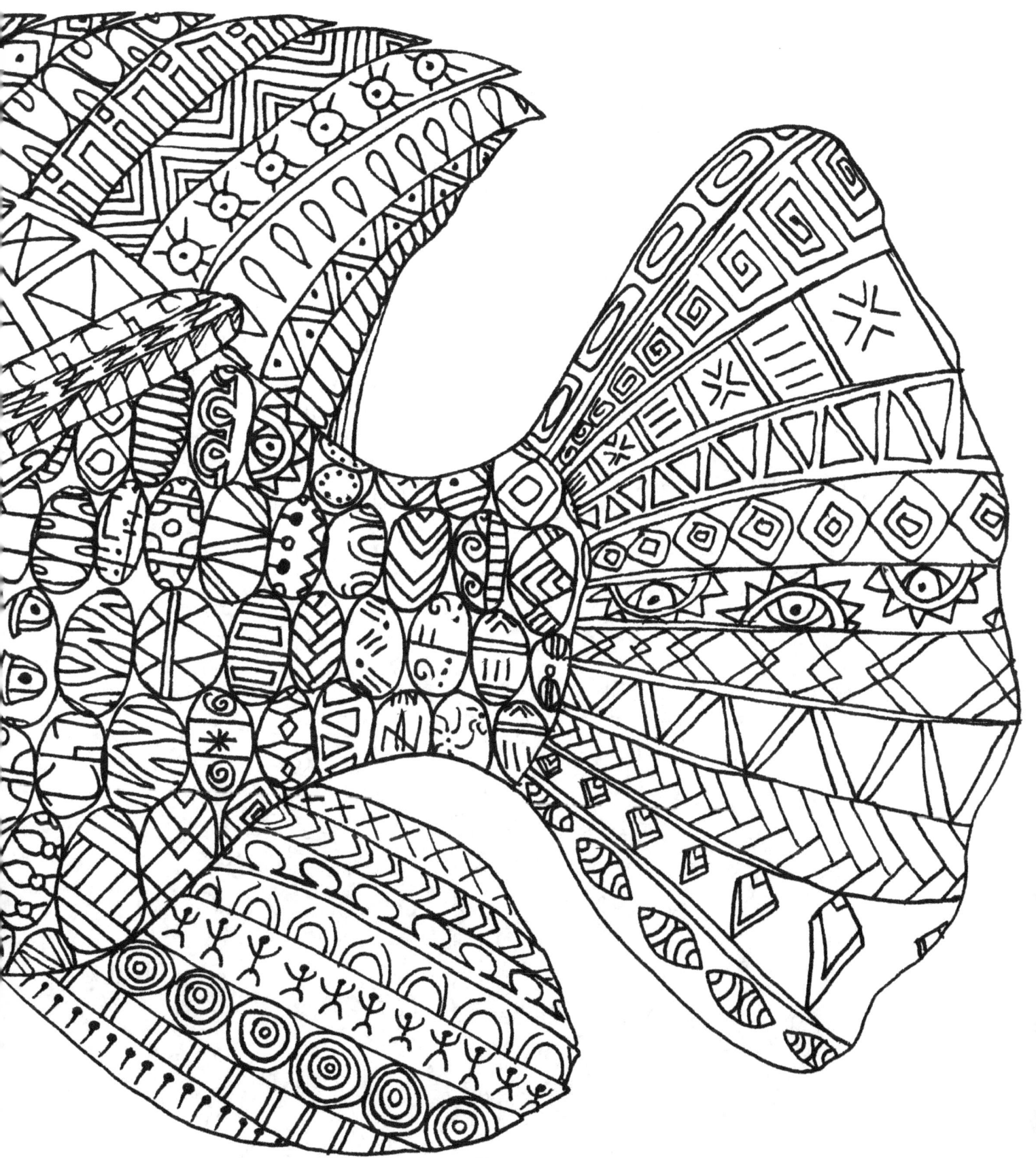

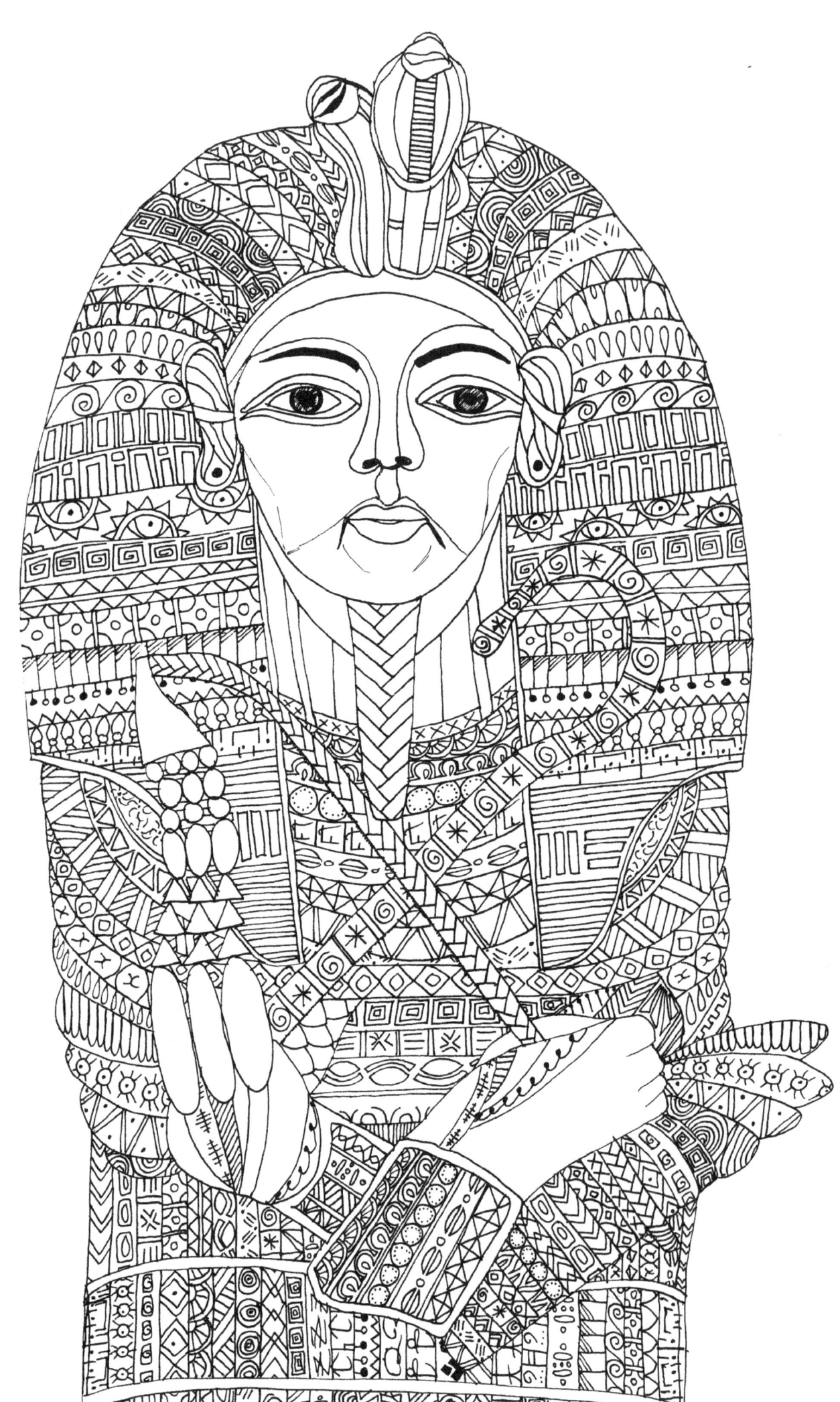

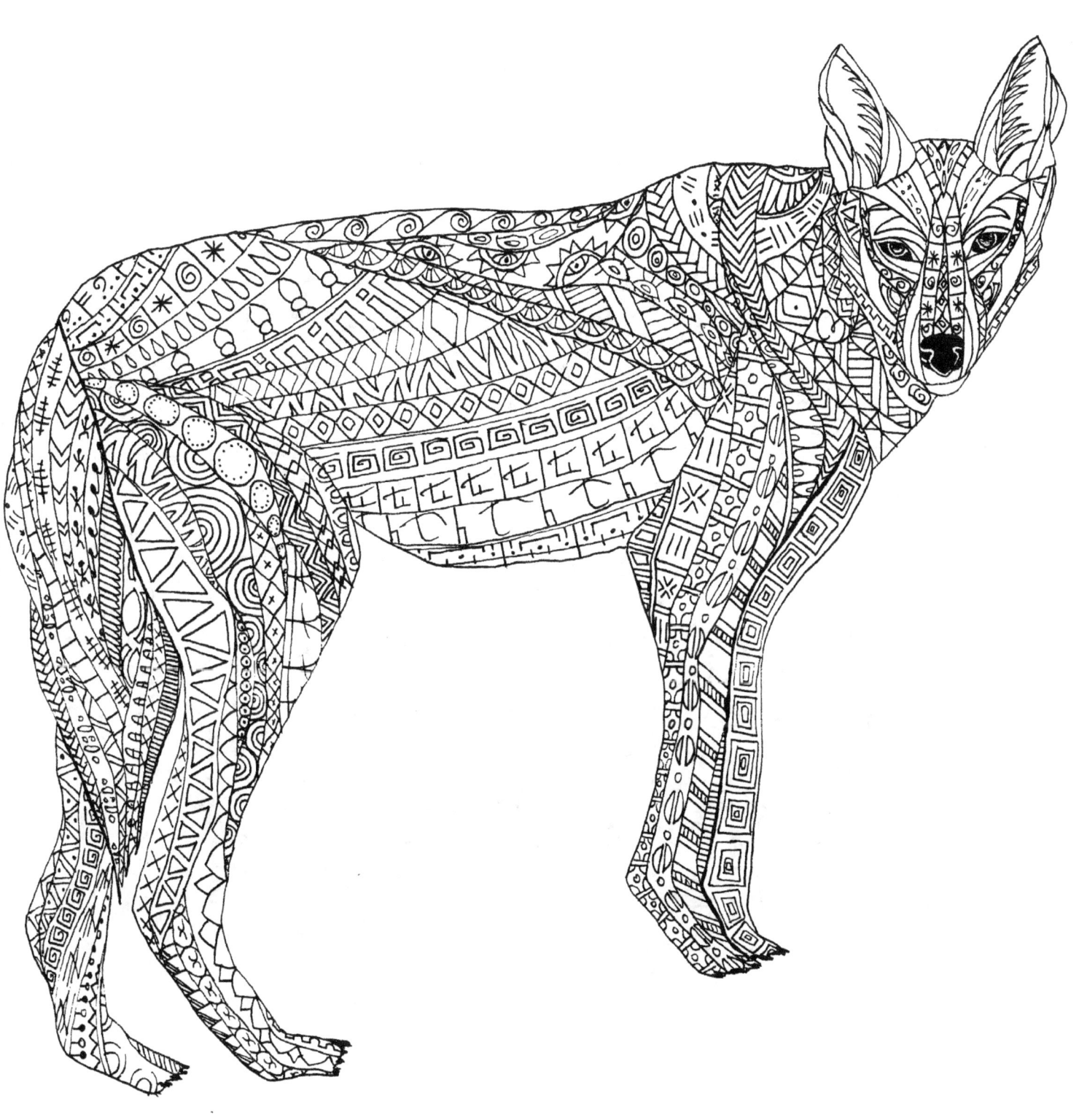

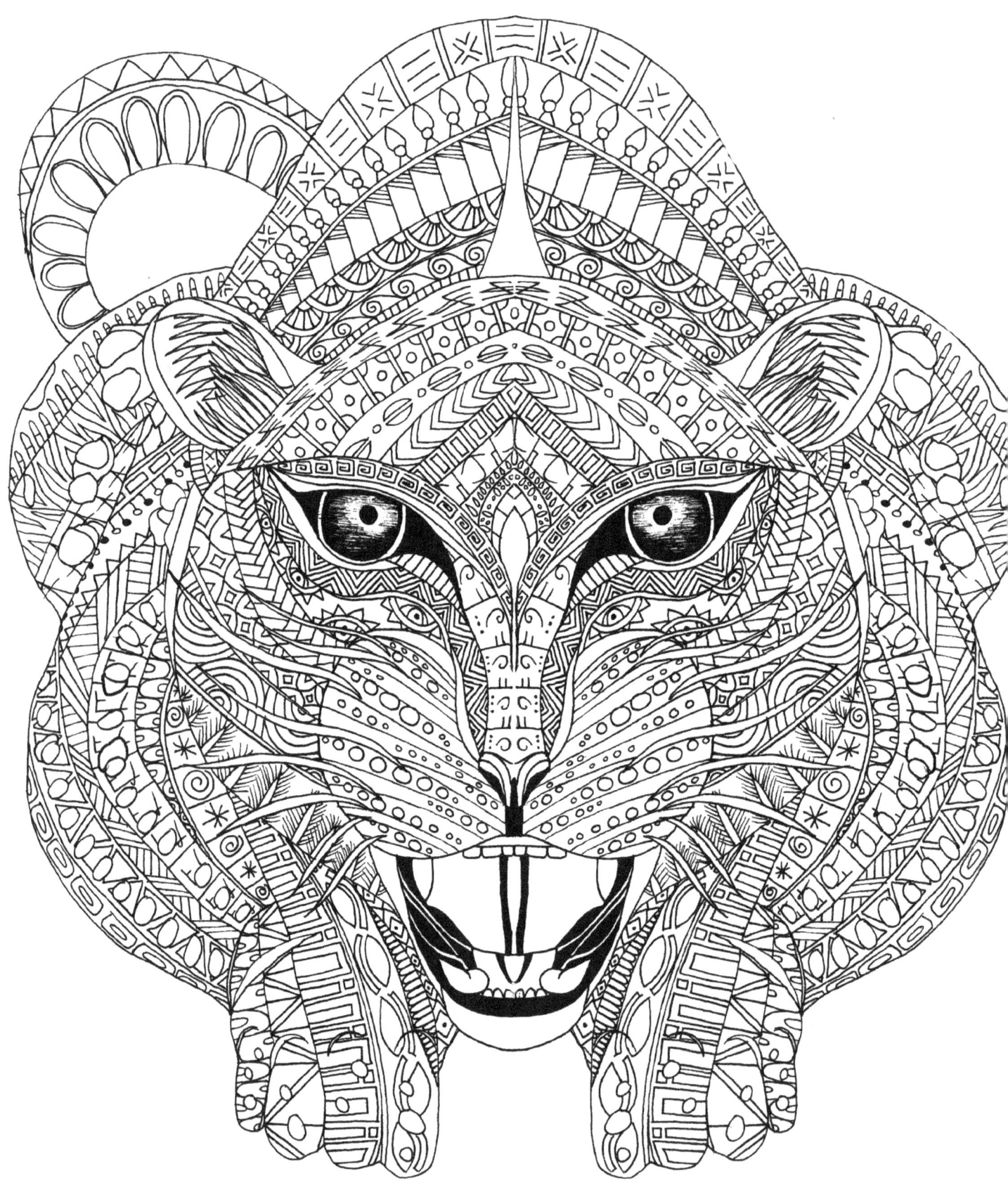

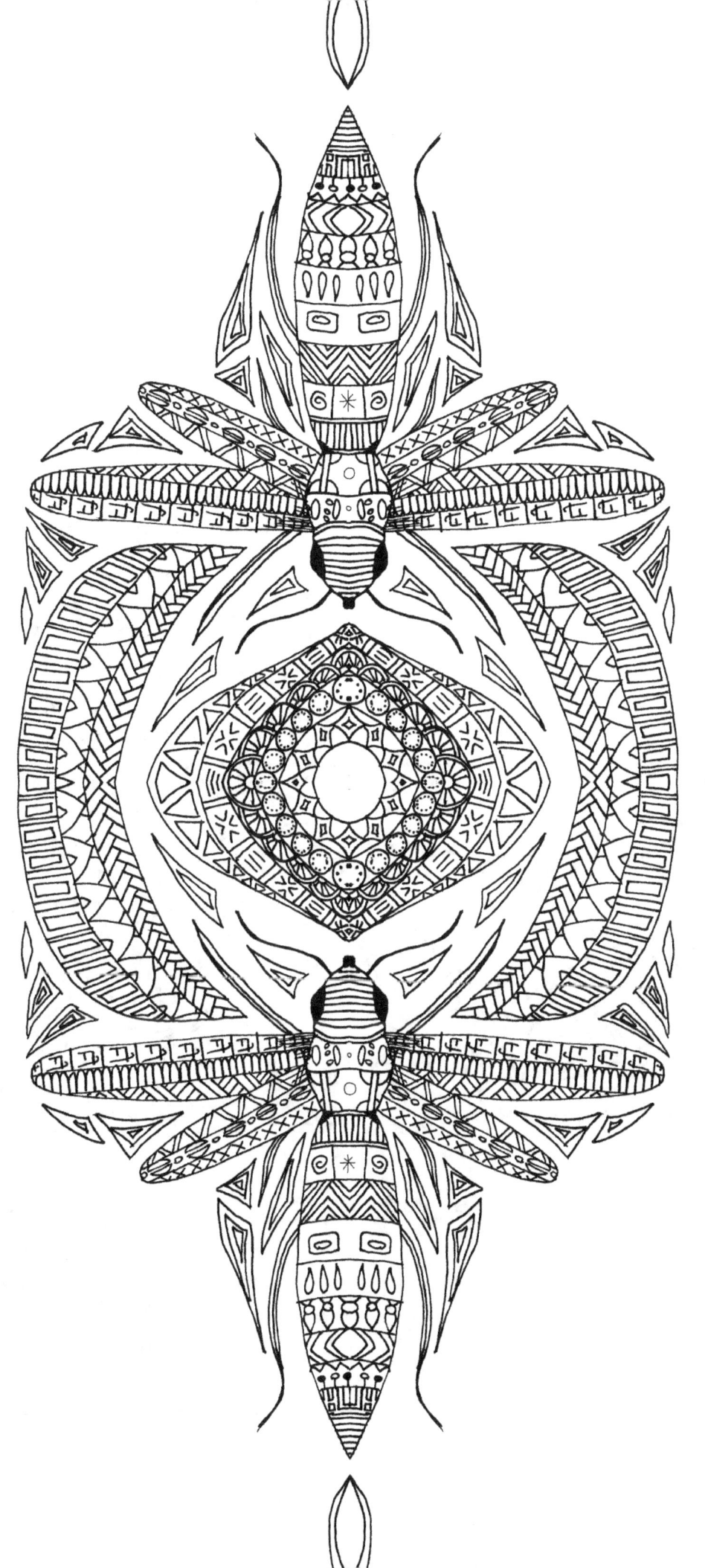

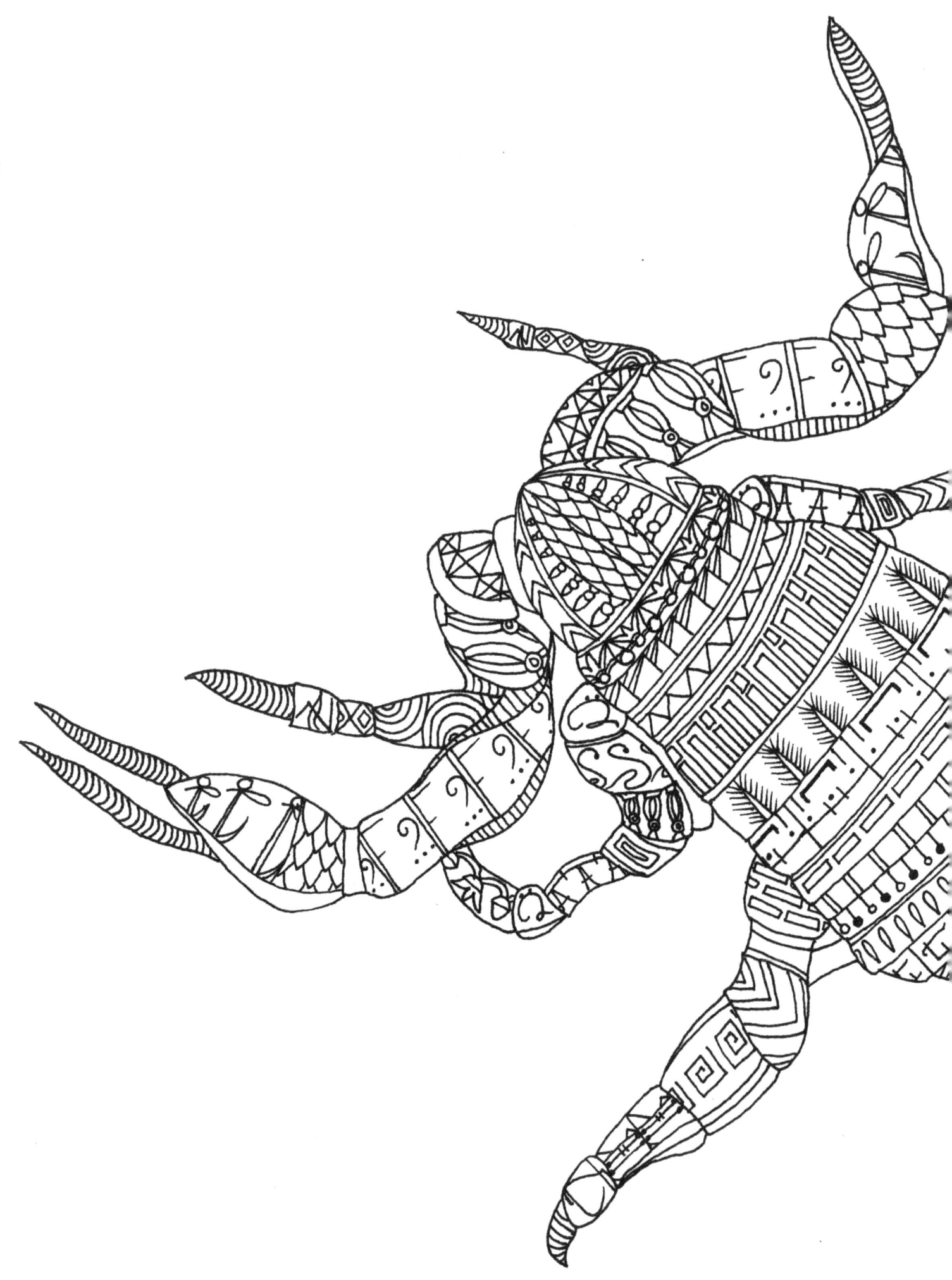

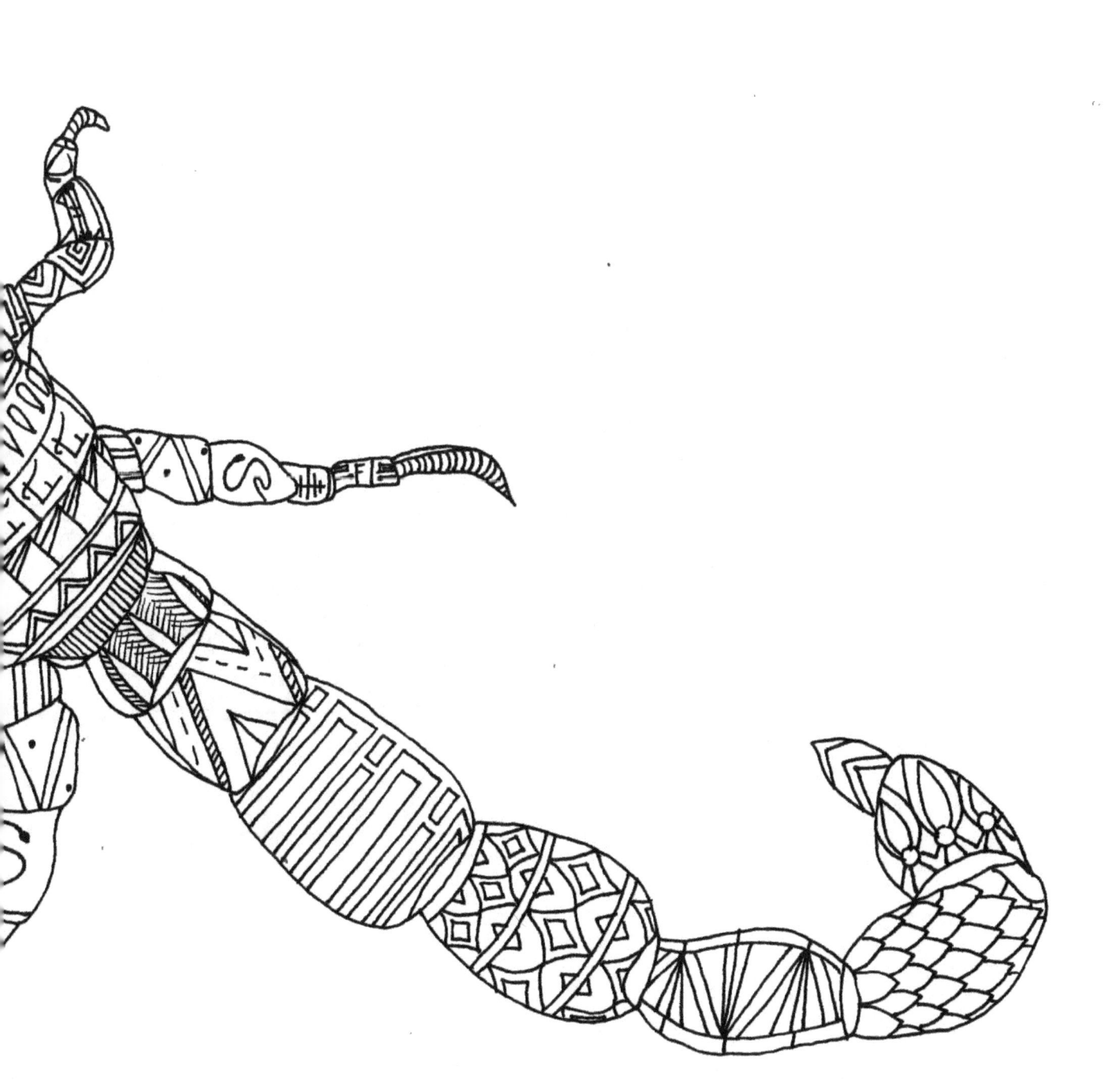

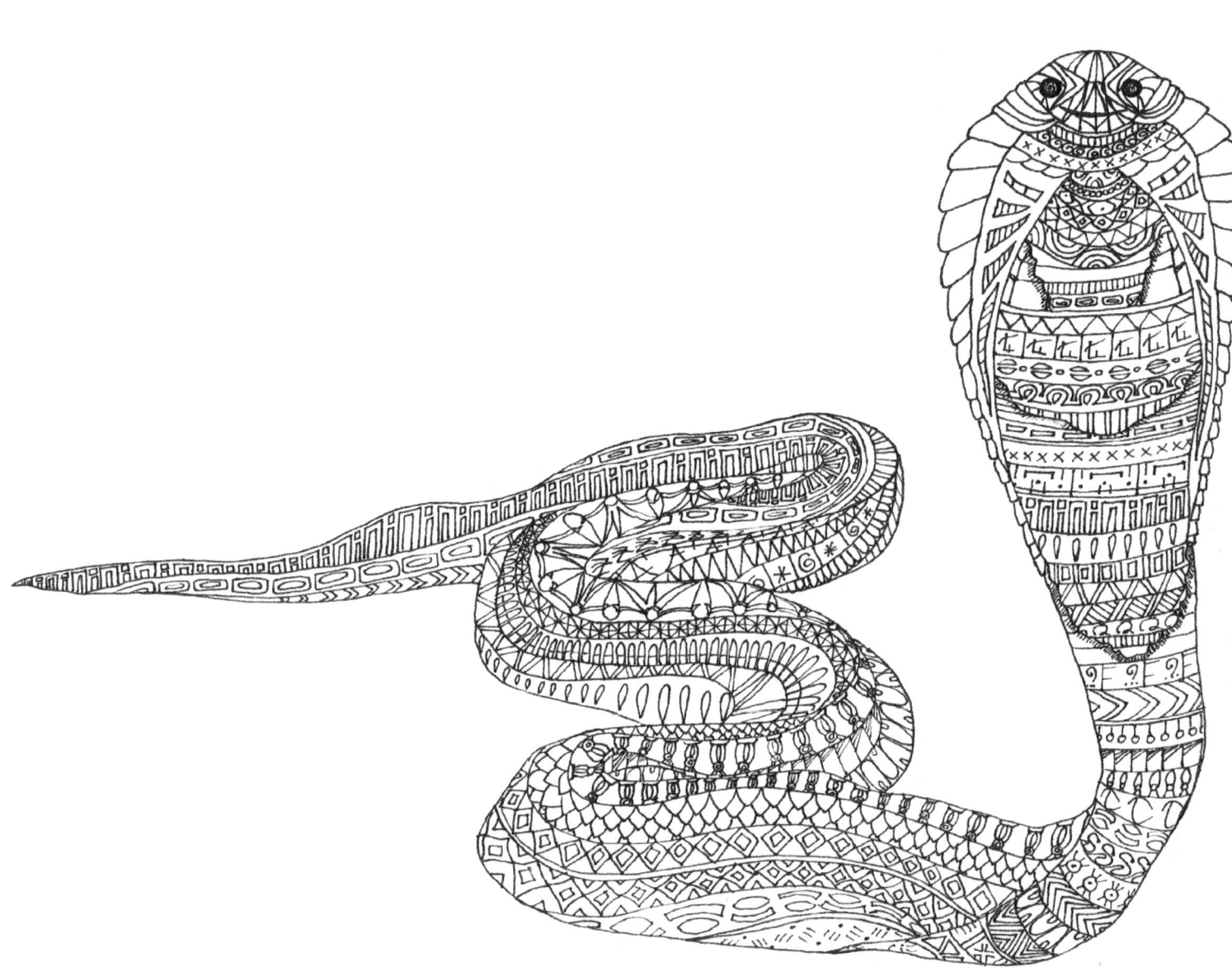

www.ingramcontent.com/pod-product-compliance
Lightning Source LLC
Chambersburg PA
CBHW082219220526
45470CB00010B/3229